Georgia CRCT Coach, GPS Edition, Social Studies, Grade 7

Coach™®

Triumph Learning®

Acknowledgments

page 33 © Komar/Shutterstock.com; page 42 © Hugo Maes/Shutterstock.com; page 60 © Dave Stamboulis/Alamy; page 83 © David Cleaves/Alamy; page 90 © Anke Van Wyk/Dreamstime.com; page 95 © Benson HE/Shutterstock.com; page 98 © Martin Harvey/Getty; page 131 © Craig DeBourbon/iStockphoto.com; page 151 © Marc van Vuren/Shutterstock.com; page 158 © Noam Armonn/Shutterstock.com; page 182 © Dariusz Kopestynski/Dreamstime.com; page 200 © Bill Perry/Shutterstock.com; page 220 © JinYoung Lee/Shutterstock.com

Georgia CRCT Coach, GPS Edition, Social Studies, Grade 7
318GA
ISBN-10: 1-60824-666-3
ISBN-13: 978-1-60824-666-3

Cover Image: Peach globe in front of the Georgia state flag. © iStockphoto.com/Duncan Walker; © iStockphoto.com/kutay tanir

Triumph Learning® 136 Madison Avenue, 7th Floor, New York, NY 10016

Table of Contents

Letter to the Student 5

Letter to the Family 6

Georgia Performance Standards Correlations Chart 7

Pretest 13

Chapter 1	**Civics, Government, and Economics**	31	
	Lesson 1	Forms of Government	32	SS7CG1.a–c SS7CG4.a–c SS7CG6.a–c
	Lesson 2	Economic Systems	36	SS7E1.a–b SS7E4, SS7E5.a–b SS7E8.a–b
	Lesson 3	Trade	42	SS7E2.a–b SS7E6.a–b SS7E9.a–b
	Chapter 1 Review	46	
Chapter 2	**Africa**	51	
	Lesson 4	Colonization of Africa	52	SS7H1.a
	Lesson 5	African Nationalist Movements	58	SS7H1.b
	Lesson 6	South Africa and Apartheid	64	SS7H1.b–c
	Lesson 7	Pan-African Movement	68	SS7H1.d
	Lesson 8	Physical Features of Africa	72	SS7G1.a–b, SS7G3.a
	Lesson 9	African Environmental Policies	78	SS7G2.a–c
	Lesson 10	Cultural Features of Africa	82	SS7G4.a–b
	Lesson 11	African Health Issues	86	SS7CG3.a–b SS7CG4.c
	Lesson 12	African Governments	90	SS7CG2.a
	Lesson 13	African Trade	94	SS7E2.a–b
	Lesson 14	African Economies	98	SS7E1.c, SS7E3.a–d
	Chapter 2 Review	102	

Chapter 3   **Southwest Asia (Middle East)** 111

    Lesson 15   Origins of Judaism, Christianity,
             and Islam 112   SS7G8.c–d

    Lesson 16   The Ottoman Empire 118   SS7H2.a

    Lesson 17   The State of Israel 122   SS7H2.b

    Lesson 18   Israeli and Arab Conflict 126   SS7H2.c

    Lesson 19   The Impact of Oil and the Southwest
             Asian Wars 130   SS7G7.a, SS7H2.d

    Lesson 20   Physical Features of Southwest Asia 134   SS7G5.a–b, SS7G7.b

    Lesson 21   Southwest Asian Environmental Policies . 140   SS7G6.a

    Lesson 22   Cultural Features of Southwest Asia 144   SS7G8.a–e

    Lesson 23   Southwest Asian Governments 150   SS7CG5.a

    Lesson 24   Southwest Asian Trade 154   SS7E6.a–d

    Lesson 25   Southwest Asian Economies 158   SS7E5.c, SS7E7.a–d

    Chapter 3 Review 162

Chapter 4   **Southern and Eastern Asia** 171

    Lesson 26   End of Colonialism 172   SS7H3.a–b

    Lesson 27   Japan After World War II 176   SS7H3.c

    Lesson 28   The Reign of Mao Zedong 180   SS7H3.d

    Lesson 29   The Korean War 186   SS7H3.e

    Lesson 30   The Vietnam War 190   SS7H3.e

    Lesson 31   Physical Features of Southern
             and Eastern Asia 194   SS7G9.a–b
                                                                    SS7G11.a–b

    Lesson 32   Southern and Eastern Asian
             Environmental Policies 200   SS7G10.a–b

    Lesson 33   Cultural Features of Southern
             and Eastern Asia 204   SS7G12.a–c

    Lesson 34   Southern and Eastern Asian
             Governments 210   SS7CG7.a

    Lesson 35   Southern and Eastern Asian Trade 214   SS7E9.a–c

    Lesson 36   Southern and Eastern Asian Economies . . 218   SS7E8.c, SS7E10.a–d

    Chapter 4 Review 222

Posttest 231

Glossary 248

Letter to the Student

Dear Student,

Welcome to the *Georgia CRCT Coach, GPS Edition, Social Studies, Grade 7*. This book will help you strengthen your social studies skills this year. *Coach* also provides practice with the kinds of questions you will have to answer on tests, including the state test.

The *Coach* book is divided into chapters and lessons. Before you begin the first chapter, you may want to take the Pretest at the beginning of the book. The Pretest will show you your strengths and weaknesses in the skills and strategies you need to know this year. This way, you will be aware of what you need to concentrate on to be successful. At the end of the *Coach* book is a Posttest that will allow you and your teacher to evaluate how much you have learned. We have tried to match the style of the state test in the Pretest and Posttest for better test practice.

The lessons in this book will help you review and practice your skills and get you ready to take tests. Some of the practice will be in the style of the state test. In general, you will be answering multiple-choice, constructed-response, and open-ended or extended-response questions. Questions like these may appear on your state test. Practicing with these types of questions will give you a good idea of what you need to review to triumph.

Here are some tips that will help you as you work through this book. Remembering these tips will also help you do well on the state test.

- Listen closely to your teacher's directions.
- When answering multiple choice questions, read each choice carefully before choosing the BEST answer.
- Time yourself so that you have time at the end of a test to check your answers.

We hope you will enjoy using *Coach* and that you will have a fun and rewarding year!

Letter to the Family

Dear Parents and Families,

The *Coach* series of workbooks is designed to help your child to master grade-appropriate skills in social studies and to take the Grade 7 CRCT, which is the test administered each year in the state of Georgia. In your state, the grade-appropriate skills are assessed using the Georgia Performance Standards. These are the skills the state has chosen as the building blocks of your child's education in social studies, and these are the skills that will be tested on the Georgia State Test. Your child's success will be measured by how well he or she masters these skills.

You are an important factor in your child's ability to learn and succeed. Get involved! We invite you to be our partner in making learning a priority in your child's life. To help ensure success, we suggest that you review the lessons in this book with your child. While teachers will guide your child through the book in class, your support at home is also vital to your child's comprehension.

Please encourage your child to read and study this book at home, and take the time to go over the sample questions and homework together. The more students practice, the better they do on the actual exam and on all the tests they will take in school. Try talking about what your child has learned in school. Perhaps you can show your children real-life applications of what they have learned. For example, you could discuss why skills are important in life.

We ask you to work with us this year to help your child triumph. Together, we can make a difference!

The *Coach* Parent Involvement Pledge

As an involved parent, I pledge to:

- promote the value of education to my child

- inspire my child to read

- discuss the skills my child needs with his or her teachers and principal

- expect my child to successfully fulfill school and homework assignments

- join in school activities and decisions

I hereby pledge my involvement in my child's educational success!

Parent Signature: _____

Student Signature: _____

SOUTHWEST ASIA (Middle East)

Standard	Description	Coach Lesson(s)	Check When Completed
SS7G5	**The student will locate selected features in Southwestern Asia (Middle East).**	20	
SS7G5.a	Locate on a world and regional political-physical map: Euphrates River, Jordan River, Tigris River, Suez Canal, Persian Gulf, Strait of Hormuz, Arabian Sea, Red Sea, and Gaza Strip.	20	
SS7G5.b	Locate on a world and regional political-physical map the nations of Afghanistan, Iran, Iraq, Israel, Saudi Arabia, and Turkey.	20	
SS7G6	**The student will discuss environmental issues across Southwest Asia (Middle East).**	21	
SS7G6.a	Explain how water pollution and the unequal distribution of water impacts irrigation and drinking water.	21	
SS7G7	**The student will explain the impact of location, climate, physical characteristics, distribution of natural resources and population distribution on Southwest Asia (Middle East).**	19–20	
SS7G7.a	Explain how the distribution of oil has affected the development of Southwest Asia (Middle East).	19	
SS7G7.b	Describe how the deserts and rivers of Southwest Asia (Middle East) have affected the population in terms of where people live, the type of work they do, and how they travel.	20	
SS7G8	**The student will describe the diverse cultures of the people who live in Southwest Asia (Middle East).**	22	
SS7G8.a	Explain the differences between an ethnic group and a religious group.	22	
SS7G8.b	Explain the diversity of religions within the Arabs, Persians, and Kurds.	22	
SS7G8.c	Compare and contrast the prominent religions in Southwest Asia (Middle East): Judaism, Islam, and Christianity.	22	
SS7G8.d	Explain the reason for the division between Sunni and Shia Muslims.	22	
SS7G8.e	Evaluate how the literacy rate affects the standard of living.	22	
SS7CG4	**The student will compare and contrast various forms of government.**	1	
SS7CG4.a	Describe the ways government systems distribute power: unitary, confederation, and federal.	1	
SS7CG4.b	Explain how governments determine citizen participation: autocratic, oligarchic, and democratic.	1	
SS7CG4.c	Describe the two predominant forms of democratic governments: parliamentary and presidential.	1	
SS7CG5	**The student will explain the structures of the national governments of Southwest Asia (Middle East).**	23	
SS7CG5.a	Compare the parliamentary democracy of the State of Israel, the monarchy of the Kingdom of Saudi Arabia, and the theocracy of the Islamic Republic of Iran, distinguishing the form of leadership and the role of the citizen in terms of voting rights and personal freedoms.	23	

Standard	Description	*Coach* Lesson(s)	Check When Completed
SS7E5	**The student will analyze different economic systems.**	2, 25	
SS7E5.a	Compare how traditional, command, and market economies answer the economic questions of (1) what to produce, (2) how to produce, and (3) for whom to produce.	2	
SS7E5.b	Explain how most countries have a mixed economy located on a continuum between pure market and pure command.	2	
SS7E5.c	Compare and contrast the economic systems in Israel, Saudi Arabia, and Turkey.	25	
SS7E6	**The student will explain how voluntary trade benefits buyers and sellers in Southwest Asia (Middle East).**	3, 24	
SS7E6.a	Explain how specialization encourages trade between countries.	3, 24	
SS7E6.b	Compare and contrast different types of trade barriers, such as tariffs, quotas, and embargos.	3, 24	
SS7E6.c	Explain the primary function of the Organization of Petroleum Exporting Countries (OPEC).	24	
SS7E6.d	Explain why international trade requires a system for exchanging currencies between nations.	24	
SS7E7	**The student will describe factors that influence economic growth and examine their presence or absence in Israel, Saudi Arabia, and Iran.**	25	
SS7E7.a	Explain the relationship between investment in human capital (education and training) and gross domestic product (GDP).	25	
SS7E7.b	Explain the relationship between investment in capital (factories, machinery, and technology) and gross domestic product (GDP).	25	
SS7E7.c	Explain the role of oil in these countries' economies.	25	
SS7E7.d	Describe the role of entrepreneurship.	25	
SS7H2	**The student will analyze continuity and change in Southwest Asia (Middle East) leading to the 21st century.**	16–19	
SS7H2.a	Explain how European partitioning in the Middle East after the breakup of the Ottoman Empire led to regional conflict.	16	
SS7H2.b	Explain the historical reasons for the establishment of the modern State of Israel in 1948; include the Jewish religious connection to the land, the Holocaust, anti-Semitism, and Zionism in Europe.	17	
SS7H2.c	Describe how land and religion are reasons for continuing conflicts in the Middle East.	18	
SS7H2.d	Explain U.S. presence and interest in Southwest Asia; include the Persian Gulf conflict and invasions of Afghanistan and Iraq.	19	

SOUTHERN AND EASTERN ASIA

Standard	Description	*Coach* Lesson(s)	Check When Completed
SS7G9	**The student will locate selected features in Southern and Eastern Asia.**	31	
SS7G9.a	Locate on a world and regional political-physical map: Ganges River, Huang He (Yellow River), Indus River, Mekong River, Yangtze (Chang Jiang) River, Bay of Bengal, Indian Ocean, Sea of Japan, South China Sea, Yellow Sea, Gobi Desert, Taklimakan Desert, Himalayan Mountains, and Korean Peninsula.	31	
SS7G9.b	Locate on a world and regional political-physical map the countries of China, India, Indonesia, Japan, North Korea, South Korea, and Vietnam.	31	
SS7G10	**The student will discuss environmental issues across Southern and Eastern Asia.**	32	
SS7G10.a	Describe the causes and effects of pollution on the Yangtze and Ganges Rivers.	32	
SS7G10.b	Describe the causes and effects of air pollution and flooding in India and China.	32	
SS7G11	**The student will explain the impact of location, climate, physical characteristics, distribution of natural resources, and population distribution on Southern and Eastern Asia.**	31	
SS7G11.a	Describe the impact climate and location has on population distribution in Southern and Eastern Asia.	31	
SS7G11.b	Describe how the mountain, desert, and water features of Southern and Eastern Asia have affected the population in terms of where people live, the types of work they do, and how they travel.	31	
SS7G12	**The student will analyze the diverse cultures of the people who live in Southern and Eastern Asia.**	33	
SS7G12.a	Explain the differences between an ethnic group and a religious group.	33	
SS7G12.b	Compare and contrast the prominent religions in Southern and Eastern Asia: Buddhism, Hinduism, Islam, Shintoism, and the philosophy of Confucianism.	33	
SS7G12.c	Evaluate how the literacy rate affects the standard of living.	33	
SS7CG6	**The student will compare and contrast various forms of government.**	1	
SS7CG6.a	Describe the ways government systems distribute power: unitary, confederation, and federal.	1	
SS7CG6.b	Explain how governments determine citizen participation: autocratic, oligarchic, and democratic.	1	
SS7CG6.c	Describe the two predominant forms of democratic governments: parliamentary and presidential.	1	

Standard	Description	*Coach* Lesson(s)	Check When Completed
SS7CG7	**The student will demonstrate an understanding of national governments in Southern and Eastern Asia.**	34	
SS7CG7.a	Compare and contrast the federal republic of The Republic of India, the communist state of The People's Republic China, and the constitutional monarchy of Japan, distinguishing the form of leadership and the role of the citizen in terms of voting rights and personal freedoms.	34	
SS7E8	**The student will analyze different economic systems.**	2, 36	
SS7E8.a	Compare how traditional, command, and market economies answer the economic questions of (1) what to produce, (2) how to produce, and (3) for whom to produce.	2	
SS7E8.b	Explain how most countries have a mixed economy located on a continuum between pure market and pure command.	2	
SS7E8.c	Compare and contrast the economic systems in China, India, Japan, and North Korea.	36	
SS7E9	**The student will explain how voluntary trade benefits buyers and sellers in Southern and Eastern Asia.**	3, 35	
SS7E9.a	Explain how specialization encourages trade between countries.	3, 35	
SS7E9.b	Compare and contrast different types of trade barriers, such as tariffs, quotas, and embargos.	3, 35	
SS7E9.c	Explain why international trade requires a system for exchanging currencies between nations.	35	
SS7E10	**The student will describe factors that influence economic growth and examine their presence or absence in India, China, and Japan.**	36	
SS7E10.a	Explain the relationship between investment in human capital (education and training) and gross domestic product (GDP).	36	
SS7E10.b	Explain the relationship between investment in capital (factories, machinery, and technology) and gross domestic product (GDP).	36	
SS7E10.c	Describe the role of natural resources in a country's economy.	36	
SS7E10.d	Describe the role of entrepreneurship.	36	
SS7H3	**The student will analyze continuity and change in Southern and Eastern Asia leading to the 21st century.**	26–30	
SS7H3.a	Describe how nationalism led to independence in India and Vietnam.	26	
SS7H3.b	Describe the impact of Mohandas Gandhi's belief in non-violent protest.	26	
SS7H3.c	Explain the role of the United States in the rebuilding of Japan after WWII.	27	
SS7H3.d	Describe the impact of communism in China in terms of Mao Zedong, the Great Leap Forward, the Cultural Revolution, and Tiananmen Square.	28	
SS7H3.e	Explain the reasons for foreign involvement in Korea and Vietnam in terms of containment of communism.	29, 30	

Georgia CRCT Coach, GPS Edition, Social Studies, Grade 7

PRETEST

Name: _____

General Instructions

Today you will be taking a test similar to the Social Studies Criterion-Referenced Competency Test. The Social Studies test consists of multiple-choice questions. A sample has been included. The sample shows you how to mark your answers. There are several important things to remember.

- Answer all questions on your answer sheet. Do not mark any answers to questions in your test booklet.

- For each question, choose the best answer, and completely fill in the circle in the space provided on your answer sheet.

- If you do not know the answer to a question, skip it and go on. You may return to it later if you have time.

- If you finish the section of the test that you are working on early, you may review your answers in that section only. You may not review another section or go on to the next section of the test.

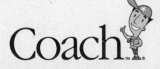

Sample Question

The sample test question below is provided to show you what the questions in the test are like and how to mark your answer to each question. For each question, choose the one best answer, and fill in the circle in the space provided on your answer sheet for the answer you have chosen. Be sure to mark all of your answers to the questions on your answer sheet.

Sample

In what country is the Yellow River located?

A. China

B. India

C. Egypt

D. Kenya

PLEASE STOP! DO NOT GO ON TO THE NEXT PAGE.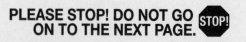

Section 1

Section 1 of this test has thirty questions. Choose the best answer for each question. Fill in the circle in the spaces provided for questions 1 through 30 on your answer sheet.

1. Which of Africa's major rivers is located in central Africa?

    A. Zambezi River

    B. Nile River

    C. Congo River

    D. Niger River

2. Why is the government of Kenya concerned with desertification and deforestation?

    A. Desertification and deforestation lead to higher taxes.

    B. Desertification and deforestation in Kenya pollute the Nile River.

    C. The people of Kenya cannot adapt to a desert climate.

    D. The people of Kenya rely on the land for their livelihoods.

3. What was the dominant religion in the Ottoman Empire?

    A. Christianity

    B. Judaism

    C. Islam

    D. Buddhism

4. Which religion do MOST people in Southwest Asia practice?

    A. Christianity

    B. Judaism

    C. Islam

    D. Buddhism

5. What happened as a result of the 1953 treaty signed at the end of the Korean conflict?

    A. victory for South Korea

    B. victory for North Korea

    C. defeat of the United States

    D. stalemate

PLEASE GO ON TO THE NEXT PAGE.

6. Outsourcing by the United States has become an important source of income in India. One reason for outsourcing is that compared to the United States, India has

A. better technology.

B. lower wages.

C. higher wages.

D. higher taxes.

7. The government of Iran today is based upon shari'ah, or Islamic law. Which term BEST describes a government based upon religion?

A. a democracy

B. a theocracy

C. an aristocracy

D. a monarchy

8. The Strait of Hormuz connects the Persian Gulf with the

A. Red Sea.

B. Mediterranean Sea.

C. Black Sea.

D. Arabian Sea.

9. Which sect of Islam believes that its leader should be a direct descendant of Muhammad?

A. Shi'a

B. Sunni

C. Kurd

D. Judaic

PLEASE GO ON TO THE NEXT PAGE.

Use the map below to answer questions 10 and 11.

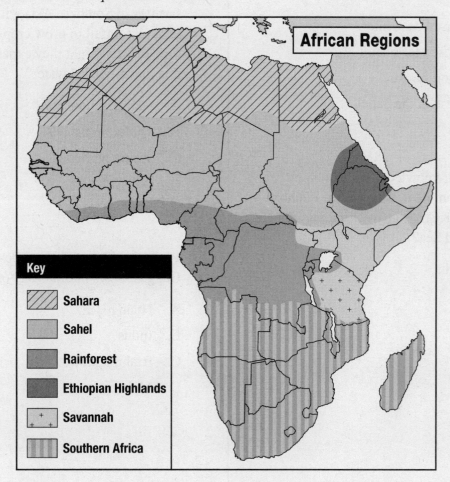

African Regions

Key

- Sahara
- Sahel
- Rainforest
- Ethiopian Highlands
- Savannah
- Southern Africa

10. The Sahara Desert covers large parts of all of following countries EXCEPT

   A. Algeria.

   B. Libya.

   C. Egypt.

   D. Ethiopia.

11. Which of the following countries has large areas of rainforest?

   A. Nigeria

   B. Kenya

   C. South Africa

   D. Sudan

PLEASE GO ON TO THE NEXT PAGE.

12. In Africa, desertification leads to

    A. increased pesticides.

    B. decreased farm land.

    C. growing forests.

    D. increase in the Sahel.

13. Using your knowledge of geography of the African continent, which is the country MOST LIKELY to have a trading influence on the Red Sea?

    A. Nigeria

    B. Chad

    C. Mali

    D. Egypt

14. Seasonal weather patterns determine when farmers in Southern Asia will receive enough rainfall to grow crops. At what time of year might they expect to receive this much-needed water?

    A. summer monsoons

    B. winter monsoons

    C. spring typhoons

    D. fall cyclones

15. Which major Asian river, besides the Ganges, flows into the Bay of Bengal?

    A. Huang He

    B. Indus

    C. Brahmaputra

    D. Mekong

PLEASE GO ON TO THE NEXT PAGE.

16. What revolutionary leader led the Communist Party to power in China in 1949?

   A. Zhou Enlai

   B. Chiang Kai-shek

   C. Emperor Hirohito

   D. Mao Zedong

17. Why does Israel NOT enjoy the benefits of the oil industry in Southwest Asia?

   A. The United Nations has placed an embargo on Israeli oil.

   B. Other countries have high tariffs on Israeli oil.

   C. Israel uses a command economy.

   D. Israel has no oil reserves.

18. What religion started in India and spread to Eastern Asia?

   A. Taoism

   B. Buddhism

   C. Islam

   D. Judaism

19. What is the organization responsible for the regulation of much of the world's oil supply and price structure?

   A. OPEC

   B. NAFTA

   C. NATO

   D. ECOWAS

PLEASE GO ON TO THE NEXT PAGE.

20. The waterway that forms a border between Jordan to the east and Israel and the West Bank to the west is the

    A. Tigris River.

    B. Suez Canal.

    C. Red Sea.

    D. Jordan River.

21. Which South African president helped bring an end to apartheid?

    A. Joseph Mobutu

    B. Jomo Kenyatta

    C. Julius Nyere

    D. Frederik Willem de Klerk

22. What has helped Israel be so successful in increasing agricultural production?

    A. recent abundant rainfall

    B. economic assistance from the United States

    C. advanced irrigation

    D. petroleum reserves

23. Which nation in Southern and Eastern Asia is made up of many islands?

    A. Bangladesh

    B. Indonesia

    C. India

    D. Vietnam

PLEASE GO ON TO THE NEXT PAGE.

24. Why is the Huang He River known as "China's Sorrow"?

    A. There is not enough water for irrigation.

    B. There is extreme water pollution.

    C. There is destructive flooding.

    D. The new dams are too expensive.

25. What is an effect of a country having a high literacy rate?

    A. a high standard of living

    B. a low standard of living

    C. a trade deficit

    D. a trade surplus

26. The Diet is the legislative branch of government in

    A. Vietnam.

    B. China.

    C. India.

    D. Japan.

27. Which of the following countries uses a parliamentary democracy form of government?

    A. North Korea

    B. China

    C. Japan

    D. India

PLEASE GO ON TO THE NEXT PAGE.

28. What is the Japanese national religion?

    A. Buddhism

    B. Hinduism

    C. Shinto

    D. Islam

29. What is the main reason that Japan imports most of the materials it needs for manufacturing?

    A. It has advanced shipping.

    B. It lacks abundant natural resources.

    C. It seeks a favorable balance of trade.

    D. It has a stable economic system.

30. At the Berlin Conference, European nations agreed to divide up the African continent. What was the main goal of the European nations?

    A. to gain control of natural resources

    B. to gain new markets for manufactured goods

    C. to gain opportunities for religious missionaries

    D. to gain land for new citizens

PLEASE STOP! DO NOT GO ON TO THE NEXT PAGE.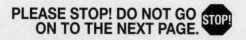

Section 2

Section 2 of this test has thirty questions. Choose the best answer for each question. Fill in the circle in the spaces provided for questions 31 through 60 on your answer sheet.

31. How would you describe the form of government in Saudi Arabia?

    A. republic

    B. monarchy

    C. democracy

    D. confederation

32. The economies of South Africa and Nigeria are

    A. mixed economies.

    B. traditional economies.

    C. command economies.

    D. market economies.

33. What is the reason for the continuing conflicts between Israel and its Arab neighbors?

    A. Israel has nuclear weapons.

    B. Israel has a high tariff on Arab goods.

    C. There are no oil reserves in Israel.

    D. Arabs and Israelis want the same land.

34. Why has Saudi Arabia assumed a lead role in the economic fortunes of Southwest Asia?

    A. because of the stability of the Saudi family

    B. because of Saudi Arabia's large share of the world's oil reserves

    C. because of Saudi Arabia's opposition to Israeli reforms

    D. because of Saudi Arabia's massive supertanker fleet

PLEASE GO ON TO THE NEXT PAGE.

35. A person who is willing to take risks to start a new business is called

   A. a manager.

   B. an entrepreneur.

   C. a banker.

   D. an inventor.

36. Seasonal winds, or monsoons, across Southern Asia affect economic production. When might the agricultural industry expect to receive needed rainfall to plant its crops?

   A. summer

   B. winter

   C. spring

   D. fall

37. The Indo-Gangetic Plain is one of the most densely populated regions of the world. In which country is it located?

   A. Pakistan

   B. Bangladesh

   C. India

   D. Indonesia

38. After North Korea tested nuclear weapons, members of the United Nations agreed to refuse to sell certain products to North Korea. What is this an example of?

   A. a tariff

   B. an embargo

   C. a quota

   D. specialization

39. What is it called when someone is loaned money for a fee?

   A. saving

   B. credit

   C. spending

   D. investing

PLEASE GO ON TO THE NEXT PAGE.

40. Which of the following is NOT one of the three major religions that originated in Southwest Asia?

    A. Islam

    B. Hinduism

    C. Judaism

    D. Christianity

41. What reason did the United States government have for entering the Vietnam conflict in the early 1960s?

    A. to assist Chinese intervention

    B. to stop the spread of communism

    C. to support Ho Chi Minh

    D. to restore rule to France

42. The Mekong Delta played an important part in American military history in the 1960s. Which two countries of Southern and Eastern Asia does the Mekong flow through?

    A. Laos and Cambodia

    B. Thailand and Myanmar

    C. Thailand and Laos

    D. Cambodia and Vietnam

43. Africa's tropical grasslands, home to an amazing variety of wildlife, are known as

    A. savannahs.

    B. deserts.

    C. rainforests.

    D. the Sahel.

44. Why is Africa affected by the AIDS epidemic more than the other continents?

    A. Africa has the greatest population, so more people are affected.

    B. Africa needs more money for education and prevention programs.

    C. Africa has the largest land mass.

    D. Africa has the warmest climate.

PLEASE GO ON TO THE NEXT PAGE.

45. The form of government in which power is held by a small, unelected group of leaders is called

A. an oligarchy.

B. a democracy.

C. a republic.

D. a dictatorship.

46. Under the leadership of Mao Zedong, China attempted to catch up to the powers of the West in industrial and agricultural production. Mao's program to accomplish this goal was called

A. the Cultural Revolution.

B. the Great Leap Forward.

C. the rise of communism.

D. the Long March.

47. What is a community of people sharing ancestry, customs, and language known as?

A. a religious group

B. an ethnic group

C. a nomadic group

D. a caste

48. Using your geographic knowledge, which country must use irrigation to maintain a growing agricultural industry outside the Indus River valley?

A. Pakistan

B. India

C. Japan

D. South Korea

49. All of these countries are considered members of the Pacific Rim EXCEPT

A. Japan.

B. Cuba.

C. China.

D. Vietnam.

PLEASE GO ON TO THE NEXT PAGE.

Use the timeline below to answer question 50.

50. Which statement BEST represents the facts in the timeline for the Ottoman Empire?

    A. The 15th century was a time of peace with few battles.

    B. Rule of the Ottomans parallels periods of war in Europe.

    C. Military reform occurred at the same time as the Near East wars.

    D. The wars in Europe ended after the Ottoman Empire fell.

PLEASE GO ON TO THE NEXT PAGE. ➡

51. What was the event that led to the United States' invasion of Iraq in the 1991 Persian Gulf War?

    A. discovery of weapons of mass destruction

    B. Iraqi missile attacks on Israel

    C. Iraqi invasion of Kuwait

    D. threat of nuclear weapons attack

52. Which term BEST explains the economic system in North Korea today?

    A. mixed

    B. market

    C. command

    D. traditional

53. In 1989, the Chinese government violently repressed a popular protest in

    A. Macao.

    B. Tiananmen Square.

    C. Taiwan.

    D. Hong Kong.

54. The strip of semi-arid land south of the Sahara Desert is known as the

    A. Sahara.

    B. Sahel.

    C. rainforests.

    D. savannah.

PLEASE GO ON TO THE NEXT PAGE.

55. How did the Mau Mau in Kenya try to gain independence from Britain?

    A. guerilla warfare

    B. passive resistance

    C. use of force

    D. civil disobedience

56. Which country lies directly west of Afghanistan?

    A. Iraq

    B. Iran

    C. Saudi Arabia

    D. Israel

57. In which of the following forms of government do citizens play an important role in choosing leaders?

    A. democracy

    B. autocracy

    C. oligarchy

    D. theocracy

58. What major problem do the people of Bangladesh face with the arrival of the summer monsoons?

    A. drought

    B. famine

    C. flooding

    D. desertification

PLEASE GO ON TO THE NEXT PAGE.

59. The system of laws created to enforce racial segregation in South Africa was known as

    A. nonviolent resistance.

    B. Pan-Africanism.

    C. nationalism.

    D. apartheid.

60. Which country's currency is based on the yen?

    A. India

    B. South Korea

    C. China

    D. Japan

PLEASE STOP! DO NOT GO ON TO THE NEXT PAGE.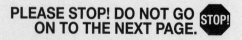

CHAPTER

1 Civics, Government, and Economics

1 Forms of Government

SS7CG1.a–c, SS7CG4.a–c, SS7CG6.a–c

Comparing Forms of Government

As of 2010, there were nearly 200 independent countries in the world. Each of these countries has its own **government**—the system it uses to make laws and run the country. While each country's government is slightly different, most fall into a few basic categories.

One way to categorize governments is by the different ways they distribute power. All countries have a central government, which is responsible for the entire country. Additional levels of government are responsible for smaller areas, such as states or provinces. In the **unitary system** of government, the central government decides which powers to grant to local governments. Local governments have important powers, but these powers are not clearly defined or protected by the country's **constitution**—a document stating the basic laws that govern a country. This means that the central government can legally limit the powers of local governments. Japan, for example, is divided into 47 prefectures, or governed districts. Each prefecture has elected leaders, but their power is limited by that of the national government.

This is different from the **federal system**, in which power is shared more evenly between the central government and the government of states or provinces. The United States uses the federal system. The powers belonging to the national government are defined in the United States Constitution. Those powers not given to the national government belong to the states and the people. This makes a state such as Georgia more powerful under the federal system than it would be under the unitary system. India is another example of a country using the federal system.

A **confederation** is a voluntary association of states in which individual states hold more power than the central government. States agree to join together to form a central government, but each state retains the power to act independently. During the American Civil War, for instance, the Confederate states joined together to form a confederation.

Citizen Participation

Another way to categorize government is to look at the role citizens play in running the government. In an **autocratic government**, power lies in the hands of a single leader. There is no limit on the power of the leader's central government. Autocratic governments do not allow elections or powerful local governments, and citizens have little chance to participate in running the country. The government of China is an example of an authoritarian system. In some **authoritarian** states, citizens play a small role in the government. In Saudi Arabia, for example, only men are allowed to vote. Voters elect some local and national leaders, but the head of the government is not elected.

Oligarchic governments are similar to autocratic governments. Rather than a single leader, however, they are led by a small group. In an oligarchy, an unelected, powerful group uses its hold over the government to enrich itself and deny power to the citizens. North Korea's government is considered an example of this system.

In contrast to autocratic and oligarchic governments, **democratic government** relies on active citizen participation. In democracies, voters choose their own leaders through elections. Citizens born in this country can also become leaders themselves. Citizens' basic rights are protected by law and cannot be taken away by individual leaders. Examples of democracies include India, Israel, and South Africa.

Citizens have the right to vote in democracies.

Forms of Democracy: Presidential vs. Parliamentary

There are two main forms of democratic government. The **presidential system** is the one that is familiar to Americans, since this is the system we use in the United States. The executive branch of the U.S. national government is headed by the president, while the legislative branch is made up of Congress. Congress includes the Senate and the House of Representatives. In a presidential system, the president is largely independent of Congress. For example, the president selects cabinet members who are not members of Congress. A **cabinet** is a group of people who advise the president and help run the government. The president also has the power to decide whether to sign a bill passed by Congress into law, or to veto, or reject, the bill. Congress can only pass a bill over the president's veto if two-thirds of both the House of Representatives and Senate vote to do so. Nigeria and Kenya are among other countries using the presidential system.

The balance of power between branches of government is different in the **parliamentary system**. In a parliamentary democracy, the executive branch is not as independent of the legislative branch as it is in a presidential democracy. Israel, for example, uses a parliamentary system. The leader of the national government is the **prime minister**. The prime minister is a member of the Knesset, Israel's legislature. He or she chooses cabinet members who are usually members of the legislature as well. Other examples of parliamentary governments include Turkey and Japan.

The prime minister and cabinet members of a parliamentary government can only remain in power as long as they maintain the support of the legislature. If the Israeli prime minister loses support in the Knesset, a new election is required to select new leaders. This does not happen in the governments using the presidential systems.

Show What You Know

Complete the chart below using information from this lesson.

Type of government	One important thing about this type of government	One example of this type of government
Unitary		
Federal		
Democratic		

Lesson Practice

DIRECTIONS
Circle the letter of the best answer for each item.

Thinking It Through

1. Which of the following terms BEST describes the government of Israel?

   A. presidential

   B. autocratic

   C. democratic

   D. oligarchic

   Israel uses a parliamentary system of government. Citizens participate in elections in which they select members of the national legislature.

2. Which of the following is true of a presidential democracy?

   A. The president is more independent of the legislature than in the parliamentary system.

   B. The president can only remain in power if his or her political party holds a majority in Congress.

   C. The president cannot veto acts of Congress.

   D. The president is selected by members of the cabinet.

   HINT *In presidential democracies, the president is not a member of the legislature.*

3. Which of the following countries uses the unitary system of government?

   A. the United States

   B. Japan

   C. India

   D. Nigeria

4. Which statement BEST describes the role of citizens in an autocratic system?

   A. Citizens vote in presidential elections.

   B. Citizens can challenge government rules in court.

   C. Citizens can join a variety of political parties.

   D. Citizens have no way to limit the power of the government.

2 Economic Systems

 SS7E1.a–b, SS7E4, SS7E5.a–b, SS7E8.a–b

Three Basic Economic Systems

In addition to having a government, each country also has its own **economy**. An economy is the way in which people meets their needs through the production, distribution, and use of goods and services. Different economic systems provide different answers for key questions facing all countries, such as: What is produced? Who should produce it? Who gets what is produced?

There are three basic economic systems: traditional economy, command economy, and market economy. A **traditional economy** is an economic system based on traditions, routines, and beliefs. In traditional economies, goods and services are generally shared among all members of the economy. Often, a traditional product is made and sold or traded at open markets. The benefit is that people play a direct role in deciding which goods and services are needed for themselves and the community. Different roles in a traditional economy are passed down through family members. This system is still used today by some tribes in Africa, such as the Kikuyu tribe of Kenya.

A local Moroccan market

In a **command economy**, the central government is in charge of deciding what goods and services are needed and how they will be produced. Government officials may even limit what jobs people can hold. The **consumer** in a command economy can choose among the goods that are produced, but he or she has little say in what gets made.

Egypt once had a command economy but is moving toward more economic freedom today. However, the Egyptian government still has some control over financial decisions in the economy. Pure command economies are now found only in politically isolated countries, such North Korea. Most of North Korea's industry and means of production are owned and run by the government.

Government plays no role in a pure market economy. A **market economy** is a system that is managed by the people. It is also known as a free market system, or capitalism. Market economies are based on supply and demand. Businesses control how much they produce, and people control how much they consume. Everyone is free to exchange goods and services without government involvement or regulation. Any person may start a business selling or making whatever he or she wants. There is no promise of success, but anyone can try.

The Real World: Mixed Economies

In the real world, most modern nations have economies that are somewhere between pure command and pure market economies. These are called **mixed economies**. In a mixed economy, people are free to control the means of production—factories, farms, stores, and more. Individuals and businesses decide what to produce, how to produce it, and how much it should cost. Individual consumers are free to purchase what they want, or to decide to produce goods or services themselves. In this way, a mixed economy is similar to a pure market economy.

Mixed economies and pure market economies are different, however, when it comes to the role of government. In a mixed economy, the government has important powers. It may regulate the amount of pollution a factory can produce, for example, or enforce laws ensuring that products are safe for consumers or set regulations that banks and other financial institutions must follow. The United States has a mixed economy where individual ownership is encouraged, but the government issues regulations. In some mixed economies, such as Saudi Arabia, the government has more power. The Saudi government controls the country's vast oil resources. Profits from oil sales fund government programs, such as education and defense.

Personal Money Management

No matter what economic system a country uses, individuals have an important role to play. We all have choices to make about how we earn, spend, save, and invest our money.

Income is money that literally "comes in" or is earned on a regular basis. For most people, income is something that comes from getting paid for doing work. Some people, however, are able to live off income from their savings or investments. Income may also come from gifts or from selling something.

Everyone has to **spend** money. Money is needed for food, shelter, and clothing. Of course, people spend money on things they want, too. Things that we want but do not need are called **luxuries**. The best way to spend money wisely is to make a **budget**, which is a plan for how much money will be spent on each type of item that a person must buy. Following a budget makes it possible for a person to plan ahead for **necessities**.

A chart like this one can be used to figure out a monthly budget.

Monthly Budget	
Income: $2000	
Item	Amount to Spend
Housing	$1200
Food	$200
Utilities	$300
Transportation	$100
Entertainment	$50
Luxuries	$150

Savings

One goal of budgeting is to save money. **Saving** allows people to plan to buy something expensive in the future. By setting aside a small amount of money every week, it is possible to save a large amount of money over time. It also creates a store of money that can be used in an emergency. The goal of saving money is either to buy something you cannot currently afford—such as a house, a car, or a college education—or to be able to stop working. When people save enough money to stop working, they can retire. Planning for retirement is the long-term savings goal of most Americans.

There are many different ways to save money. You can keep money in a piggy bank, but it is best to save money in a secured financial institution such as a bank or credit union. In a bank, your money can earn interest. **Interest** is a charge that the bank pays you to use your money. Although you can get your money at any time, the bank is using your money in various ways. For this privilege the bank pays you a percentage of the amount that you have saved. The amount of interest paid ranges from less than 1% to as much as 14%.

If $10 is placed in a bank account that earns 5% interest per year, then 5% of the total balance of the account is added to it on a regular basis. Over time, this helps the money grow. Read the chart below.

Bank Balance	5% Interest Added
$10.00 in start of first year	$0.50 at the end of first year
$10.50 in start of second year	$0.53 at the end of second year
$11.03 in start of third year	$0.55 at the end of third year
$11.58 in start of fourth year	$0.58 at the end of fourth year

Notice that the bank balance started with $10 and no new money is put into the bank, except interest. If the person with the bank account does not take the money out and just lets the interest add up, the balance will continue to grow. Earning interest on interest is called **compound interest**.

Investing and Credit

Money that is saved does not have to be used to retire or buy something expensive. It can also be used to invest. **Investing** is spending money in the hope of earning more money than is spent. One example of an investment that many seventh graders might have is a set of collectible trading cards. A card that is bought for $1 may someday be worth $10. That is a very good return on investment of $9—which is 900%. Almost no investments make such a good return.

The biggest investment most people make is in a home. Stocks and bonds are another kind of investment that many people make. Stocks and bonds are investments of money in companies. If the company does well, the stock increases in value and is worth more. If it does poorly, the stock decreases in value and is worth less. Every kind of investment involves such risk. A risk is the possibility of losing money that has been invested. Often, the greater the risk of losing the money, the greater the possible return will be if the investment does well.

When savings and income are not enough to pay for what a person wants or needs, he or she can use credit. **Credit** is money that you borrow from a bank. When you let the bank use your money, the bank pays you interest. When you use the bank's money, you then must pay the bank interest. The same compound interest that worked in your favor in a savings account will work against you when you borrow money. If you only pay off the interest on a credit card, you may never be able to pay off the total amount borrowed on that card. This fact is why it is important to borrow only when absolutely necessary, and pay back borrowed money as quickly as possible.

There are many different types of credit—credit cards, home loans, and student loans are just a few of the most common types. Even electricity service and phone service are types of credit because the service is offered before money is paid. Anytime money is owed, credit has been extended.

The key to personal finance is never to borrow more than you can pay off in a reasonable amount of time. Learning to control and understand personal finance is the job of every adult.

Show What You Know

Complete the chart below. Begin by selecting three of the following forms of economy: traditional, command, market, mixed. Then fill in information about each type of economy using what you read in this lesson.

Type of economy	The role of individual people in this type of economy	The role of the government in this type of economy

Lesson Practice

Thinking It Through

1. Which of the following represents an economy that is entirely controlled by a country's government?

    A. market economy

    B. command economy

    C. mixed economy

    D. traditional economy

    There are very few economies in the world today that are controlled by the government. Most economies today are mixed economies, with some government and some market control.

Use the list below to answer question 2.
*   goods are shared by the whole community
*   economy is based on customs
*   roles are passed down through family members

2. Which kind of economy is described by the features listed above?

    A. mixed

    B. market

    C. traditional

    D. command

    HINT *Some tribes in Africa still use this form of economy.*

3. Which is NOT an example of personal income?

    A. compounding interest

    B. salary

    C. return on investment

    D. credit

4. Which of the following BEST describes the purpose of making a budget?

    A. for spending money on luxuries

    B. for saving money or planning for expenses

    C. for creating credit card debt

    D. for investing in stocks

3 Trade

 SS7E2.a–b, SS7E6.a–b, SS7E9.a–b

Benefits of Trade

Trade is defined as the exchange, purchase, or sale of goods and services. International trade is based on the importing and exporting of goods and services. The total value of international trade is now more than $25 trillion a year. **Exports** are products that one country sends to another. **Imports** are products one country buys from another.

International trade has benefits for both buyers and sellers throughout Asia and Africa. Car factories in Japan, for example, are able to earn money by selling their goods in other countries. Buyers all over the world benefit as well, by gaining a larger option of cars to choose from.

Most nations specialize in producing certain goods or services. According to the theory of **specialization**, each country produces goods that it is able to make efficiently. Specialization leads to increased international trade because countries are able to earn money selling the things they are good at making. At the same time, countries want to buy goods they are not able to produce at home.

Some countries specialize in a certain product because of the country's natural resources. For example, Saudi Arabia has the largest oil reserves in the world. So it is not surprising that Saudi Arabia specializes in producing oil. Since Saudi Arabia is able to produce large amounts of oil efficiently, other nations want to buy this product from them. Saudi Arabia can then use the money it earns to import goods that are produced more efficiently in other countries.

International trade increases wealth around the world.

Trade Barriers

Sometimes countries limit what can be traded to their people. Governments try to use these limits, called **trade barriers**, to protect their businesses from foreign competition. There are several types of trade barriers.

A **tariff**, or a tax on imports, is one type of barrier. By taxing imported goods, a country can protect the goods made in its own country. The tax will make an imported good cost more.

Another type of trade barrier is an **import quota**, which limits the number of goods that can be imported from a certain country. It has a similar effect to tariffs, because it makes a certain item harder to get. When things are rare, their price increases.

Another type of trade barrier is an **embargo**—a ban on trade with a certain country. Embargoes are normally used for political, not economic, reasons. After Iraq's invasion of Kuwait in 1990, the United Nations imposed a strict embargo on Iraq. The embargo banned nearly all trade with Iraq, with the goal of pressuring Iraqi leader Saddam Hussein to withdraw his forces. The embargo remained in place until 2003, following the fall of Hussein's government.

Some trade barriers are part of the physical environment. Africa's Sahara Desert and Asia's Himalayan Mountains are two examples. Since moving goods across deserts and over mountains can be difficult, these features act as natural trade barriers.

Trade Agreements

Countries often work to increase trade by making trade agreements with other countries. These agreements remove trade barriers and increase wealth in countries by opening new markets and creating jobs.

Free trade is trade without tariffs or other trade barriers. Countries sign free trade agreements in the hope that open trade will benefit all the economies involved in the agreement. Ten countries in Southern and Eastern Asia, for example, have joined in the Association of Southeast Asian Nations (ASEAN) Free Trade Area. ASEAN countries work together to increase trade between members by eliminating tariffs and other trade barriers.

Currency Exchange Rates

The countries of Asia and Africa use a huge variety of currencies. A **currency** is a system of money—the currency of the United States, for example, is the dollar. In order for countries with different currencies to trade, a **currency exchange rate** must be used. The currency exchange rate compares one country's currency to another. It tells people in one country how much their money is worth in countries using different currencies.

One U.S. dollar (USD) is not equal to one Japanese yen. In the fall of 2009, the dollar–yen exchange rate was 1 dollar = 88 yen. This currency exchange rate changes from day to day. Each country has a different exchange rate with every other country. The only way to find out an up-to-date currency exchange rate is to check with a bank or a currency exchange service or on the Internet.

The currency exchange system allows foreign trade to happen. Without currency exchange rates, countries would not know how much money to charge for the goods they export. They would not know what to pay for goods they import. Additional examples of different currencies are the Indian rupee, the Israeli shekel, and the South African rand.

Show What You Know

Describe the reasons a country might want to expand its trade with other countries.

_____

_____

_____

_____

_____

_____

_____

_____

_____

_____

_____

_____

_____

_____

_____

_____

Lesson Practice

DIRECTIONS
Circle the letter of the best answer for each item.

Thinking It Through

1. Which statement BEST describes how the currency exchange helps international trade?

    A. It acts as a trade barrier between nations.

    B. It is easy to use because it never changes.

    C. It only allows trade among countries that border each other.

    D. It tells people how much their currency is worth in other countries.

    The exchange rate is constantly changing. It helps all nations trade, regardless of location.

---

2. Saudi Arabia specializes in the production and export of

    A. cars.

    B. computers.

    C. wheat.

    D. oil.

    HINT *Saudi Arabia's most valuable export is a natural resource.*

3. A ban on trade with a certain nation is called

    A. a quota.

    B. an embargo.

    C. a tariff.

    D. a free trade agreement.

4. A tax on imports is called

    A. a quota.

    B. a tariff.

    C. an embargo.

    D. a sale.

Review

Choose the best answer for each question. Fill in the circle in the spaces provided on your answer sheet.

1. In which form of government are citizens free to participate in deciding who runs the country?

    A. totalitarian

    B. democratic

    C. oligarchic

    D. autocratic

2. Which is the BEST description of an oligarchic form of government?

    A. Government power is concentrated in the hands of a single leader.

    B. Citizens control the government through regular elections.

    C. Power is evenly balanced between central and local governments.

    D. A small group of unelected leaders controls the government.

3. Sara earned $400 doing part-time jobs. She wants to buy a computer that costs $450. Her father told her to put the money into the bank where it will earn interest. This is an example of which economic activity?

    A. earning

    B. saving

    C. borrowing

    D. crediting

4. A "market economy" is

    A. an economy in which free markets determine what gets manufactured and sold.

    B. an economy in which the government creates plans for what will be produced.

    C. an economy in which people trade for whatever is available.

    D. an economy in which both the government and producers decide what to sell.

Use the map below to answer questions 5 and 6.

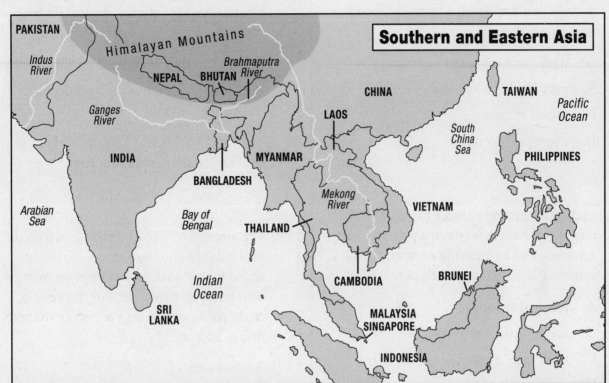

5. Which feature shown on the map acts as a natural trade barrier?

   A. Indian Ocean

   B. Ganges River

   C. Mekong River

   D. Himalayan Mountains

6. Which country can benefit from the Ganges River?

   A. India

   B. China

   C. Vietnam

   D. Cambodia

7. In which type of economy does the government decide what to produce and how to produce it?

   A. traditional economy

   B. pure market economy

   C. mixed economy

   D. command economy

8. Like most countries, India has an economy that is somewhere between a pure market economy and a command economy. India's economy is BEST described as a

   A. planned economy.

   B. mixed economy.

   C. traditional economy.

   D. free market economy.

9. Which of the following is true of a confederate government?

   A. The central government has more power than the states.

   B. The states must always act together.

   C. The government is made up of a voluntary association of states.

   D. It is an autocratic form of government.

10. Which of the following is the result of paying only the interest charged on your credit card?

    A. The credit card is paid off too quickly.

    B. The credit card is paid off over the course of many years.

    C. The credit card can never be paid off.

    D. The credit card is cancelled.

11. The amount of money charged on a credit card balance and the amount of money added by the bank to a savings account both build up over time. For this reason, credit cards and savings accounts are both said to accrue

    A. budgets.

    B. incomes.

    C. risks.

    D. compounding interest.

12. One main reason countries sign trade agreements is to

    A. remove trade barriers between countries.

    B. protect businesses from foreign competition.

    C. limit trade between countries.

    D. determine the exchange rate between currencies.

13. Japan ships billions of dollars worth of cars and trucks to other countries each year. For Japan, motor vehicles are a valuable

    A. export.

    B. tariff.

    C. import.

    D. embargo.

14. Which is the BEST definition of "specialization"?

    A. Each country sets laws about what can be imported.

    B. Each country's currency has a different value.

    C. Each country produces the goods it is able to make most efficiently.

    D. Each country makes all the goods it needs.

15. A tax on imports is called

    A. a quota.

    B. a tariff.

    C. an embargo.

    D. a sale.

16. In 1990, the United Nations banned trade with Iraq in response to Iraq's invasion of Kuwait. This ban was an example of

    A. a tariff.

    B. a voluntary trade restriction.

    C. a quota.

    D. an embargo.

Read the statement below to answer question 17.

A nation's prime minister loses support in the legislature. A new election must be held to allow citizens to select a new national leader.

17. In which form of government could the above situation take place?

   A. parliamentary democracy

   B. autocratic government

   C. presidential democracy

   D. confederate government

18. Which of the following is true of the currency exchange rate?

   A. It is only used by countries in Asia and Africa.

   B. It is no longer an important tool in international trade.

   C. It remains the same from day to day.

   D. It tells you how much your currency is worth in countries using different currencies.

19. Spending money in the hope of earning more money than is spent is called

   A. saving.

   B. investing.

   C. budgeting.

   D. credit.

Read the statements below to answer question 20.

The president is the leader of the executive branch of government.

The president is largely independent of the legislature.

20. Which form of government is described above?

   A. presidential democracy

   B. authoritarian regime

   C. parliamentary democracy

   D. oligarchy

21. In a unitary government

   A. the central government can limit the power of local governments.

   B. local governments are free to ignore national laws.

   C. the national constitution protects the rights of local governments.

   D. a single leader controls all levels of government.

CHAPTER

2 Africa

4 Colonization of Africa

 SS7H1.a

Beginning more than 1000 years ago, the people of Africa established many large empires. Empires such as Ghana, Mali, and Ethiopia became important centers of trade and learning.

Europeans were attracted by the valuable trading opportunities in Africa. By the mid-19th century, Europeans had explored and mapped most of Africa. Steamships and railroads allowed Europeans to travel into the continent. This sparked an age of colonialism. **Colonialism** is the forced control of one nation by another nation.

The Slave Trade

European powers wanted to colonize Africa for many reasons. One reason was to use enslaved Africans as a source of labor in European colonies.

When Europeans first began to colonize the Americas in the 1500s, they used Native Americans for slave labor. Diseases, however, decreased the population of enslaved Native Americans dramatically. The Native Americans had no immunity to the diseases the colonists carried. As a result, many Native Americans died. By the mid-1600s, colonists in the Americas had turned to Africa as a new source of labor.

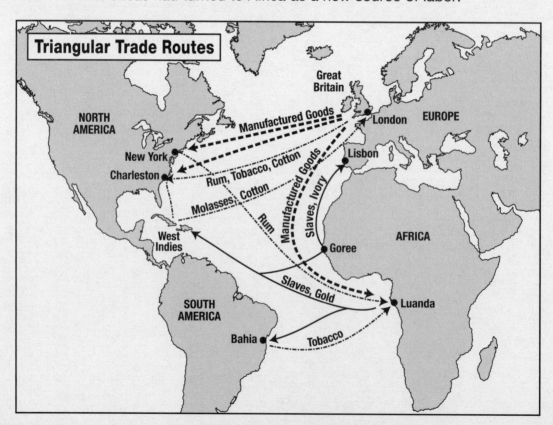

A pattern of trade known as **triangular trade** occurred between Europe, the Americas, and Africa. In one leg of the triangle, merchants from Europe brought manufactured goods to trade for captured and enslaved Africans. Africans were traded for items such as guns and cloth from Europe, and rum and gunpowder from the American colonies. Another part of the trade triangle was known as the Middle Passage. Enslaved Africans were transported from Africa to the West Indies on crowded, dangerous ships. They were traded for sugar, molasses, and other products in the Americas. These agricultural goods were then shipped to Europe and European colonies, making up the third leg of the trade triangle.

A Dutch ship that landed in Jamestown, Virginia, in 1619 was the first known slave ship in North America. The ship left Africa carrying 100 Africans, but arrived in Jamestown with only 20. It was common for people to perish on slave ships. Often the ships carried hundreds of people in dangerous conditions. They were chained together by their hands and feet. The people were held in spaces that were only tall enough to sit in, so they were unable to stand up. Illness spread quickly in the slave ships, and many Africans died in transit between Africa and the colonies. By the late 1700s, nearly 6 million Africans had been taken from their homes and transported to the Americas.

Additional Reasons for Colonization

Africa's vast natural wealth was another reason Europeans wanted to control the continent. Africa has many raw materials such as cotton, rubber, ivory, and minerals that are not found in Europe. South Africa is rich in diamonds and gold. New industries in Europe needed metals like tin and copper. Africa was rich in these, too. In addition, African countries were new markets for European goods. Europeans wanted to keep a positive trade balance. A **trade balance** is the difference in value between a country's imports and exports. The trade balance is positive when exports are greater than imports.

Colonizing Africa made it possible to create secure trade routes for European countries. The **Suez Canal** was the most important trade route. It is a human-made water route between Europe and Asia. The Suez Canal is located in Egypt and was completed in 1869. Before its construction, ships had to travel around the entire continent of Africa.

The Suez Canal was used for trade.

Europeans also wanted to change African culture to be more like European culture. Africans had their own religions. European Christians sent missionaries to Africa. A **missionary** is a person who goes to a foreign country to spread his or her religion. Missionaries brought Christianity to Africa. They also tried to end the slave trade.

Beginnings of New Imperialism

The end of the 19th century is called the age of **New Imperialism**—a fierce competition between European countries for land and power. The growth of European colonies in Africa is called the **Scramble for Africa**.

Great Britain and France fought for control of the region. The British took control of the Cape Colony from the Dutch in the early 1800s so that the French could not control it. The British also controlled some forts in West Africa, which gave them control of the ivory and gold trade. In addition, Britain took control of the Suez Canal and Egypt.

France wanted to increase its trade. It also wanted to spread French culture. By 1848, the French established themselves in northern Algeria, their first African colony. Trade outposts were built in West Africa for the slave trade.

Belgium was also competing for African land. King Leopold II purchased the Congo River basin with money from investors. The amount of land purchased was bigger than Belgium itself. The king wanted to make sure that other European countries could not control this region.

The **Berlin Conference** was a series of meetings in Berlin, Germany, held by European nations from 1884 to 1885. Africa's rulers did not attend. The European nations discussed Africa's land and how they wanted it to be divided. Ten percent of Africa was in European hands going into the meeting. When the meeting ended, Europeans had divided most of Africa into European colonies.

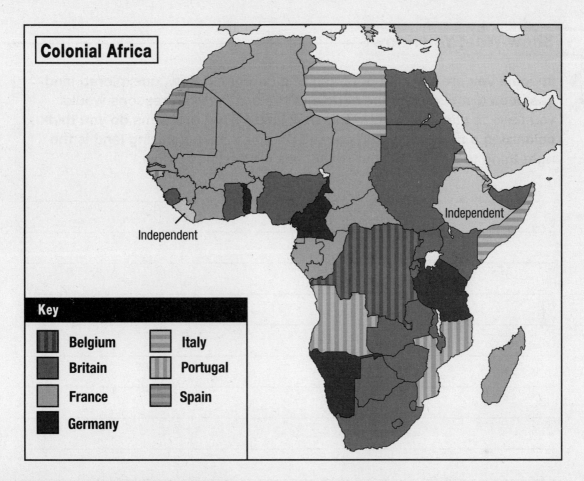

Colonial Africa

Independent

Independent

Key

Belgium

Britain

France

Germany

Italy

Portugal

Spain

Impact of Partitioning

There were some positive changes made by the colonization of Africa. Schools, hospitals, and roads were built. The Berlin Conference also set an end date for the slave trade.

The partitioning of Africa, however, contributed to long-term conflicts all over the continent. The African tribes had no control over their own countries. Land was taken to give farms to the Europeans living there. Wars, riots, and protests were common. Starvation and disease also occurred. Africans often were forced into labor.

When Europeans divided the continent, new borders were drawn. These artificial boundaries served Europeans, but were disastrous for Africans. Families and tribes were often separated, and wars were fought between tribes that used to be friendly. While most of Africa has since gained its independence, conflicts caused by the partition of Africa continue to be a problem today.

Show What You Know

Imagine you are the king or queen of a country. A new, unexplored land has been discovered in the middle of the ocean. What reasons would you have to start a colony in this new land? What problems do you think colonizing a new land might cause? Do you think colonizing land is the right thing to do? Write your responses on the lines below.

_____

_____

_____

_____

_____

_____

_____

_____

_____

_____

_____

_____

_____

_____

_____

_____

_____

_____

_____

Lesson Practice

Thinking It Through

1. In the 18th and 19th centuries, Britain and France competed for control of Egypt. What was the purpose of their competition?

   A. to control Egypt's vast oil resources

   B. to provide land to their growing populations

   C. to use Egypt's military power against the Muslims

   D. to control the trade routes between Europe and Asia

   Without the Suez Canal, boats from Europe had to travel around the entire continent of Africa to reach Asia. The Suez Canal made trade easier and faster. Nations can improve their economies by increasing trade.

2. What was the reason for the European colonization of Africa?

   A. Europeans wanted to see African wildlife.

   B. European cities were overcrowded.

   C. Europeans wanted raw materials not available in Europe.

   D. Europeans were tired of wars.

   HINT *Colonization is an economic decision by a country.*

3. Which destination was MOST common for enslaved Africans?

   A. Zambia

   B. Australia

   C. India

   D. the Americas

4. One major negative impact of the European partitioning of Africa was

   A. the construction of new hospitals.

   B. the independence of African countries.

   C. the wars between tribes that used to be friendly.

   D. the construction of the Suez Canal.

5 African Nationalist Movements

 SS7H1.b

By the early 20th century, European countries had colonized almost all of Africa. The only independent countries left were Liberia and Ethiopia. Liberia was founded in 1822, mostly by black American former slaves. However, Africans wanted to control their own governments and the continent's natural resources for their own good. In the second part of the 20th century, African nations worked to free themselves from European control. **Nationalist movements** are movements that seek independence for the people living in a country.

Kenya

Many Kenyans thought the British had taken their land unfairly. A group of Kenyans started the **Mau Mau**, which operated from 1952 to 1960. The Mau Mau was a secret society. It believed force was the only way to win Kenyan rights and independence. The Mau Mau rebelled against the British.

The British Army mostly defeated the Mau Mau by 1954, although violence continued until 1960.

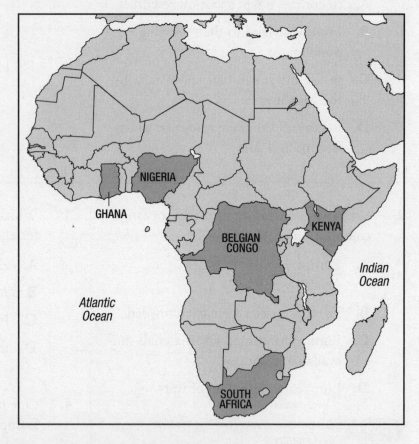

Thousands of Africans were killed in the fighting, compared to about 100 Europeans. Still, the Mau Mau movement maintained a great deal of support among Kenyans. Eventually, their support convinced the British they would have to grant independence to Kenya. The British helped Kenyans hold democratic elections. Kenyans elected Jomo Kenyatta president in 1963. On December 12, 1963, Kenya became independent once again.

Kenyatta, however, did not allow people who disagreed with him into the government. This repression caused problems in governing Kenya peacefully. Many ethnic groups fought for control of the region. Daniel arap Moi became president of Kenya in 1978. He remained president throughout the 1980s and held elections in the 1990s. However, those elections were not honest. Many countries charged Moi with mistreating Kenyans. In 2002, Moi retired. Kenya then had free elections and is more stable today than it has been in decades.

Nigeria

There were many different ethnic groups in the region now called Nigeria. An **ethnic group** is a cultural community of people with common ancestry, often sharing common religion, language, and traditions. At the Berlin Conference in 1884–1885, Britain was given control of the region, which was made into two colonies. Many of the ethnic groups did not wish to be part of the same country. These divisions among the Africans led to different treatment by the British. The British government spent more money building roads and schools in the south than in the north.

By the 1940s, Nigerians had formed many groups to fight against British rule. Some groups shared ethnicity. Some were youth and student groups. Some were made up of people who worked in the same type of job. Many people in these groups had gone to school in Europe. They admired European culture, but they believed that the only way for Nigerians to have their rights was to be free of European rule. These groups became political parties that worked for Nigerian independence.

In the late 1940s and 1950s, the British let Nigerians elect their own people into government. Abubakar Tafawa Balewa became prime minister in 1957. Great Britain gave Nigeria independence on October 1, 1960. Balewa became the first head of government. Nigeria did not have to fight for its independence from Britain.

After independence, the many ethnic groups in the region often fought each other. The main conflict existed between the northerners, who were Islamic, and the southerners, who were not Islamic. The Nigerian military took over the country in 1966.

The military ruled for many years. When free elections were held in 1993, the military ruler of the country declared them null and void. He and his successor, Sani Abacha, were especially brutal and corrupt. In 1999, civilian rule returned with the election of Olusegun Obasanjo to the presidency. Today, Nigeria has had three national elections. International groups think that the elections may not have been completely democratic. However, political and social conditions in Nigeria have improved.

South Africa

South Africa is the southernmost country in Africa. More Europeans settlers came to South Africa than to anywhere else on the continent. This fact had a strong impact on South Africa's road to independence.

In the 17th century, the Dutch were the first Europeans to settle in South Africa. Fighting among European nations for power in South Africa grew in the 19th century. Gold and diamonds were discovered in the region. The British and Dutch fought for control of these valuable resources. South Africans tried to fight the Europeans, but had no success. By the early 20th century, the British military gained control of South Africa.

South Africa's National Party supported racial segregation.

Black South Africans were not allowed to vote under British rule. This decision was the beginning of apartheid. **Apartheid** means "separateness" in Afrikaans, the language of the descendants of the Dutch settlers (or Afrikaners). Laws created to enforce segregation of people by race were called "apartheid" in South Africa. Apartheid allowed many Europeans to grow wealthy and powerful, while millions of South Africans suffered.

South Africa's white-only National Party, which came to power in 1948, was a strong supporter of apartheid. Another goal of the National Party was independence from Britain. In a white-only election in 1960, voters approved independence. The former British colony became the Republic of South Africa on May 31, 1961. The battle over apartheid would intensify in the post-independence years.

Ghana

Africans started nationalist movements in the British colony of the Gold Coast in the 1800s. It was called the Gold Coast because its land is rich in deposits of gold. The nationalist groups wanted Africans to have the same rights as the British. They also wanted to protect their land from colonists.

Nationalism increased in the Gold Coast after World War II. Many Ghanaians protested for their independence. In 1948, police fired on a group of protesters. The protestors had fought in World War II for the British. They were protesting because the government had not paid them. The police shootings of protestors led to riots in the region. Many people went on strike or protested.

In 1954, a man named Kwame Nkrumah formed a new government. His government included many Africans. In 1956, his government called for independence. The Gold Coast was renamed Ghana, after the ancient African kingdom which had been nearby. On March 6, 1957, Ghana won its independence.

The Belgian Congo

From 1885 to 1908, King Leopold II of Belgium ruled the Congo. He ran it as his own private colony. It was called the Congo Free State. It had many natural resources, such as diamonds, gold, cotton, coffee, and rubber.

Although slavery had ended in 1885 at the Berlin Conference, Africans were forced to work in mines and plantations, which were run with cruelty and even torture. Many Congolese died doing this work. Under King Leopold II, the population of the Congo Free State went from 20–30 million down to about 8 million people.

Other countries complained about the working conditions in the Congo Free State. This forced the government of Belgium to take the land from their king in 1908. It was renamed the Belgian Congo. Conditions improved, but Congolese were not allowed to run their own government. The Belgian Congo was finally granted independence in 1960, during the same year in which many other African nations won their independence.

Show What You Know

Pretend that you were born in Nigeria, South Africa, Kenya, or Ghana. Explain why you might want your country to be independent from European rule. What do you want to happen when your country is independent? What kind of rule would you like to live under? Write your ideas on the lines below.

_____

_____

_____

_____

_____

_____

_____

_____

_____

_____

_____

_____

_____

_____

_____

_____

_____

_____

_____

_____

_____

Lesson Practice

DIRECTIONS
Circle the letter of the best answer for each item.

Thinking It Through

1. Why did Africans want independence from European powers?

   Africans wanted to make decisions based on their own laws and benefit from the natural resources of their regions.

   A. European languages were confusing.

   B. They did not like Europeans.

   C. They wanted to fight each other instead of Europeans.

   D. They wanted control of their own governments.

2. What did the African nationalist movements fight for?

   A. wealth

   B. colonies

   C. independence

   D. new friends

   HINT *Their countries were controlled by foreign governments.*

3. Which of the following groups suffered MOST in Kenya's Mau Mau Rebellion?

   A. Africans

   B. British

   C. Belgians

   D. Americans

4. After independence from Great Britain, what was the Gold Coast renamed?

   A. Ghana

   B. Kenya

   C. Congo Free State

   D. Liberia

6 South Africa and Apartheid

 SS7H1.b–c

Life Under Apartheid

European colonization in South Africa led to the oppression of Africans. Many fair-skinned Europeans believed dark-skinned Africans were less than human, or simply inferior humans to themselves. This belief system is called **racism**, which is the belief that one type of ethnicity is better than another. There is no scientific basis to the idea that human beings are divided into "races," but this idea has been common for the past 150 years. The rise of slavery is one explanation for the rise of the false concept that people belong to different "races."

Under South Africa's system of apartheid, people were legally classified by the color of their skin. The racial classifications were: white, black, Asian, and colored (mixed race). The majority of South Africans were classified as black.

People of different races had to use separate services and buildings. They had separate schools, hospitals, beaches, and libraries. People of different races could not share drinking fountains or restrooms. The services and buildings for whites were much better than those for everyone else. During apartheid, white people in South Africa lived in better conditions than those found anywhere else in Africa.

Blacks suffered the most during apartheid, even though they made up the majority of the population. The government even took their citizenship away. They were forced to move to homelands and could not vote. **Homelands** were poor, crowded areas far away from cities. Homelands often did not have water or electricity. Although these areas were named "homelands," most black South Africans had never actually lived there before.

Black South Africans could only leave their homeland if they were going to work for a white person. To be allowed to come and go, black residents of homelands had to have passes. Black South Africans had to carry passes at all times. Traveling without a pass could result in going to jail.

The Anti-Apartheid Movement

In order to protest their treatment, black South Africans formed groups like the **African National Congress (ANC)**. The ANC was founded in 1912. The goal of the ANC was to bring people of all ethnicities together and to fight for rights and freedoms.

In 1944, Nelson Mandela founded the **ANC Youth League**. The purpose of the ANC Youth League was to bring a new generation to the fight against racism and apartheid. During the 1950s and 1960s, groups like the ANC received support from many groups and nations outside South Africa. In many parts of the world, apartheid was viewed as racist and unjust. In 1973, the United Nations defined apartheid as a crime against humanity. A **crime against humanity** is an international law term referring to a serious attack on human dignity or grave humiliation or a degradation of one or more human beings.

Nelson Mandela and Frederik Willem de Klerk

Nelson Mandela was an anti-apartheid activist. For many years, Mandela protested nonviolently against apartheid. Then, Mandela became leader of the ANC's armed wing in 1961. Police arrested Mandela on August 5, 1962. He was imprisoned for 27 years.

While in prison, Mandela continued to fight against apartheid. In a 1964 court appearance, he said:

During my lifetime I have dedicated myself to this struggle of the African people. I have fought against white domination, and I have fought against black domination. I have cherished the ideal of a democratic and free society in which all persons live together in harmony and with equal opportunities. It is an ideal which I hope to live for and to achieve. But if needs be, it is an ideal for which I am prepared to die.

Frederik Willem de Klerk

Mandela's imprisonment brought apartheid to the attention of the international community. Because most of the international community condemned apartheid, South Africa's political situation deteriorated. Frederik Willem de Klerk, president of South Africa, granted the release of Nelson Mandela from prison in 1990. De Klerk also ended the laws against the ANC. De Klerk agreed to end apartheid and spoke in support of a multiracial, democratic South Africa.

Mandela and De Klerk helped craft a plan to reshape South Africa. Homelands were abolished, and all citizens 18 years of age and older were granted the right to vote. When the country held an election to select a new government in 1994, Mandela and the African National Congress won more than 60% of the vote. Mandela became the first president to be elected democratically in South Africa. He was also South Africa's first black president.

Nelson Mandela served as president until 1999. Since then, South Africa has held several more elections. In 2009, long-time ANC activist Jacob Zuma was elected the country's new president. South Africa continues to face many challenges, but its transition from apartheid to democracy has gone more smoothly than many expected.

Show What You Know

Think about what you have learned about the experience of South Africa under apartheid. Respond to the following questions. What are the problems with racial segregation? How was the white minority able to maintain control of South Africa? How did the creation of homelands support this plan?

_____

_____

_____

_____

_____

_____

_____

_____

_____

_____

_____

_____

_____

_____

_____

_____

_____

_____

_____

_____

_____

_____

_____

Lesson Practice

Thinking It Through

1. Under apartheid, people of different races had to do all of the following EXCEPT

    A. register their race with the government.

    B. work with people of different races.

    C. live only with people of their own race.

    D. use separate services and buildings.

    Apartheid laws classified people by race and forced strict segregation of the races.

2. Why did South Africans form the African National Congress (ANC)?

    A. to unite South Africans to fight for greater civil rights for blacks

    B. to draw more Europeans to South Africa to oppress black people

    C. to promote segregation between blacks and whites

    D. to force white Europeans out of the homelands

    HINT *Black South Africans were oppressed by white South Africans under apartheid.*

3. Who is Nelson Mandela?

    A. the leader of the National Party

    B. the first European to arrive in South Africa

    C. the first president elected by democratic election in South Africa

    D. the last president during apartheid

4. Which statement BEST summarizes Frederik Willem de Klerk's role in recent South African history?

    A. De Klerk formed a pro-apartheid political party.

    B. He had Nelson Mandela arrested and jailed.

    C. De Klerk worked with Nelson Mandela to end apartheid.

    D. He was elected president in 2009.

7 Pan-African Movement

 SS7H1.d

Civil war and genocide are problems that have affected many African countries since the second half of the 20th century. **Civil war** is fighting between two or more regions or groups in the same country. The Democratic Republic of Congo, for example, has been torn by civil war twice since achieving independence in 1960. **Genocide** is the preplanned murder of an entire national, racial, political, or ethnic group. When civil war erupted in Rwanda in 1994, approximately 800,000 Rwandan civilians were killed by genocide.

Pan-Africanism

While African nations have suffered the tragedies of war, there have also been powerful unifying forces at work. A movement called Pan-Africanism spread across the globe during the 20th century. **Pan-Africanism** is the idea that there is a global African community made up of native Africans and the descendants of African slaves and migrants across the world.

The origins of the Pan-African movement can be traced back to the early 19th century when black intellectuals called for self-governance. The influential African American leader W.E.B. Du Bois was an early supporter of the movement. Du Bois and other leaders called for unity among all people of African descent.

As more and more African nations gained independence, the Pan-African movement rallied African nations to work together. In 1963, leaders of 32 independent African nations joined to form the Organization of African Unity (OAU). One goal of the OAU was to support ongoing nationalist independence movements. The OAU also worked to end civil wars in Africa and to find resolutions to wars between nations.

OAU members were very active in pressuring South Africa to end apartheid. One important tool in this struggle was the support of international economic sanctions against South Africa. **Economic sanctions** include policies such as trade restrictions and embargoes. They are used by one or more countries to punish or pressure another country. International economic pressure was a key factor in forcing South Africa to change.

The African Union

Another lasting impact of the Pan-African movement was the creation of a new and more powerful international organization in Africa. Members of the OAU wanted to achieve greater cooperation between nations on a variety of issues, including political and economic challenges. In 2001, members of the OAU voted to form the African Union. The **African Union (AU)** is an organization of 53 African nations that work together for peace and security. The organization works to build a strong economy, encourage democracy, and safeguard human rights all over Africa.

Every African nation except Morocco participates in the African Union. The constitution of the AU even invites the representatives of the African diaspora to participate in the organization. A **diaspora** refers to any people or ethnic group that must leave their homeland, and as a result is dispersed throughout other parts of the world. African Americans would be considered part of the African diaspora.

Today, the African Union is working toward building a central bank and a human rights court that will have authority over all African nations. The African Union is also taking direct action to protect people caught in the middle of conflict and war. In the war-torn country of Somalia, for example, AU members began a peace mission in 2007. More than 5,000 AU peacekeeping forces have been sent to Somalia. Their mission is to protect citizens and distribute humanitarian aid, such as food and medicine. The long-term goal of the AU is to help Somalia establish a stable, democratic government.

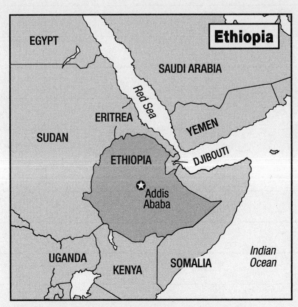

The African Union's headquarters is located in Addis Ababa, Ethiopia.

Show What You Know

Suppose you were asked to attend a meeting of the African Union. What are the three goals you think should be the AU's top priorities in the years ahead? Give your reasons.

_____

_____

_____

_____

_____

_____

_____

_____

_____

_____

_____

_____

_____

_____

_____

_____

_____

_____

_____

_____

_____

_____

_____

Lesson Practice

DIRECTIONS
Circle the letter of the best answer for each item.

Thinking It Through

1. How were 800,000 Rwandan civilians killed in 1994?

   A. disease

   B. genocide

   C. border disputes

   D. atomic bomb

   The Hutu tribe of Rwanda and Burundi planned a mass murder of Tutsis. The planned mass murder of an ethnic group is called genocide.

2. What did the Pan-African movement call for among black people?

   A. genocide

   B. unity

   C. disease

   D. food

   HINT *The Pan-African movement was aimed at people of African descent, no matter where they lived.*

3. Goals of the Organization of African Unity included all of the following EXCEPT

   A. democratic governments.

   B. continuing apartheid.

   C. ending civil wars.

   D. supporting independence.

4. What action has the African Union taken in Somalia?

   A. joined the civil war

   B. refused to get involved

   C. sent peacekeeping forces

   D. called for economic sanctions

8 Physical Features of Africa

 SS7G1.a–b, SS7G3.a

Africa is the world's second largest continent. It is home to 54 countries, 1,000 different languages, and nearly one billion people. The one thing that all African nations have in common is their reliance on the land's physical characteristics, which affect where people live and the type of work they do. The continent can be broken into many different regions: the Sahara, the Sahel, the Ethiopian Highlands, the savannahs, the rainforests, the Great Lakes, and southern Africa.

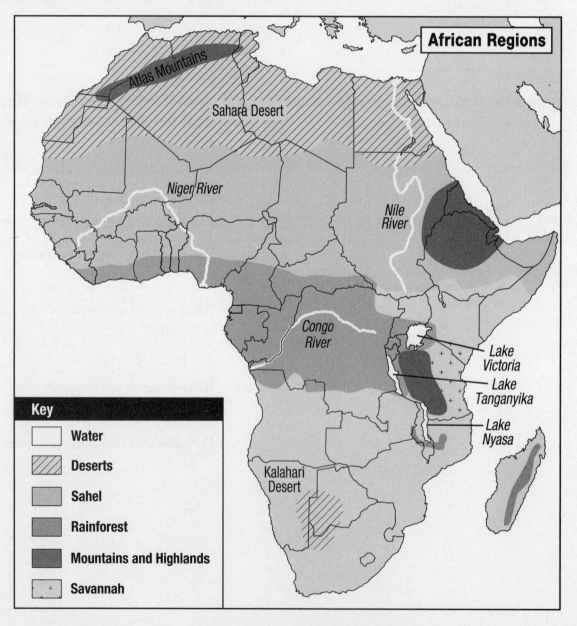

African Regions

Atlas Mountains

Sahara Desert

Niger River

Nile River

Congo River

Lake Victoria

Lake Tanganyika

Lake Nyasa

Kalahari Desert

Key

	Water
	Deserts
	Sahel
	Rainforest
	Mountains and Highlands
	Savannah

The Sahara

The **Sahara** is the world's largest desert. It is bordered on the north by the **Atlas Mountains**, a mountain range that stretches from southwest Morocco to northern Tunisia. The mountain range acts as a barrier between the desert, the Mediterranean Sea, and the Atlantic Ocean.

Because of its location between the Mediterranean Sea and the more populous areas of Africa, the Sahara Desert has historically been a trade route. **Nomadic** traders crossed the Sahara on camelback to transport goods between European and African nations.

One of the most populous areas of the Sahara region is Cairo, Egypt. Egypt is connected to Asia by the Sinai Peninsula, which makes it an important trade center. The Suez Canal allows transport through the peninsula. The **Nile River**, which is the world's longest river, provides another important waterway for transporting people and goods. It also provides a source of irrigation for agriculture.

Libya is also in the Sahara region. Libya was once a poor and politically weak nation. However, beginning in 1958, oil was discovered there. Because Libya is on the coast, it has been able to export its oil easily to other nations across the globe. Libya's economy is based on the production and export of oil.

Morocco is another nation that has benefited from its coastal location. Its rainy coastal areas produce olives, citrus fruit, and grapes. Morocco is the world's largest phosphate supplier. It also exports iron ore, silver, zinc, gold, and coal.

The Sahara region is defined by its climate, not by its national borders. Several countries straddle both the Sahara Desert and a region called the Sahel. Among them are Mauritania, Chad, Sudan, and Mali.

The Sahel

The **Sahel** is a strip of semi-arid land south of the Sahara. Some areas of the Sahel are rich in natural resources. Chad has natural reserves of gold, uranium, and oil. However, because of internal conflict and poor living conditions, most people do not gain much from the profits of these exports.

Because it depends on farming, the Sahel region can be devastated by bad weather. In the 1970s, the area suffered a drought. Almost 200,000 people died from starvation. The famine prompted many people to give up farming and move to the cities. However, the region's cities are too poor to accommodate the population increase. Many people continue to live without electricity, running water, or proper sewers.

Like Egypt, Sudan relies on the Nile River for irrigation of its crops. Sudan lies within both the Sahara and Sahel regions, so it has many different kinds of environments including forests, plateaus, grasslands, and desert. It is able to support a range of crops. The Sudanese raise livestock and grow cotton, peanuts, wheat, dates, and sugar cane.

Ethiopian Highlands

The **Ethiopian Highlands** are a rugged, mountainous region that covers parts of Ethiopia, Eritrea, and Somalia. The mountains are divided by the Great Rift Valley, a geological **fault system** that stretches 3,000 miles, from Asia to Africa.

Ethiopia is one of the poorest nations in the world. Ethiopians largely depend on **subsistence farming**. However, deforestation, bad farming practices, and drought have often led to food shortages. The nation's main export is coffee. The country is landlocked and has a very poor network of roads, which also hampers trade.

The Savannah

Africa's **savannahs**, which are tropical grasslands with scattered trees, are home to an amazing variety of wildlife. The most famous savannah is the Serengeti, a migration area for 1.5 million animals like buffalo, gazelles, and zebras.

The Serengeti includes parts of Kenya, where people rely on the land for their livelihood. About one-third of the country is grazing land for cattle, goats, and sheep. Many Kenyans make a living growing coffee and tea, which are the country's major exports.

Tropical Rainforests and the Great Lakes

Western Africa is home to a **tropical rainforest**, which is a dense evergreen forest with an annual rainfall of at least 60 inches. Unfortunately, the rainforest has shrunk substantially because of deforestation and destructive farming practices.

Part of the rainforest is in Ghana, an agricultural and mining nation. Ghana's most profitable crop is cocoa. It also has a long history as a gold and diamond exporter. Poorly maintained roads make transportation difficult in Ghana, which has slowed the growth of the timber industry.

Rainforest covers almost two-thirds of the land in the Democratic Republic of Congo, where the economy is based on oil production. Neighboring Rwanda's economy is based more on farming.

Rwanda and the Congo are also considered to be part of the Great Lakes region, along with Burundi, Uganda, Tanzania, and Kenya. There are 15 lakes in this region. Lake Victoria (bordered by Uganda, Kenya, and Tanzania) is the largest. Lake Tanganyika (located between the Democratic Republic of the Congo and Tanzania) is the deepest. The Congo River, which feeds into Lake Victoria, is the second longest river in Africa.

Southern Africa

At the southern tip of the continent is South Africa, a major producer of gold, coal, diamonds, and platinum. Despite having these natural resources, many South Africans live in poverty. Wealth from the mining industry has historically been controlled by a white minority. People of color are often paid very little. Bordering South Africa is Zimbabwe, another gold exporting nation. Another notable feature of the region is the Kalahari Desert, which covers 360,000 square miles.

Population Distribution

Africa's physical features affect where people live. The map below shows where people live in Africa.

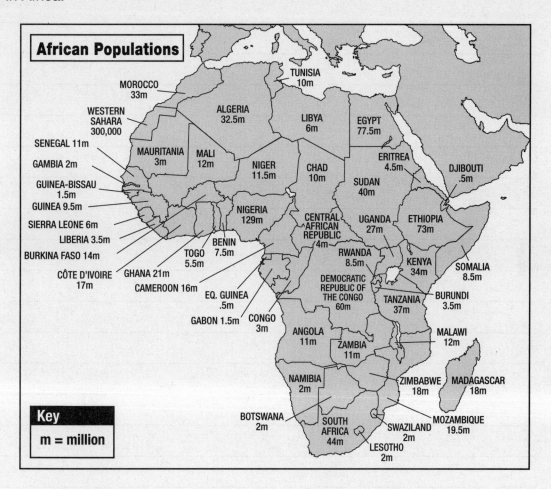

Show What You Know

Describe at least two physical characteristics that can affect where people live, the type of work they do, or how they get around in the African areas discussed in the lesson.

_____

_____

_____

_____

_____

_____

_____

_____

_____

_____

_____

_____

_____

_____

_____

_____

_____

_____

_____

_____

_____

_____

Lesson Practice

DIRECTIONS
Circle the letter of the best answer for each item.

Thinking It Through

1. What physical feature is important to Egypt's trade?

   A. the Atlas Mountains

   B. the Nile River

   C. the Sahel

   D. Lake Victoria

   Egypt's trade relies on waterways. Products must be transported by boat from Egypt to other continents.

2. What is the largest lake in Africa?

   A. Lake Niger

   B. Lake Victoria

   C. Lake Tanganyika

   D. Lake Ghana

   HINT *The lake is named for a British queen.*

3. How has Libya benefited from its location?

   A. It is far from any desert area.

   B. It shares a long border with South Africa.

   C. Its location on the coast makes trade easier.

   D. It is home to the Nile River.

4. Thick forests and high rainfall are features of Africa's

   A. Sahel.

   B. savannah.

   C. desert.

   D. tropical rainforests.

African Environmental Policies

SS7G2.a–c

Water Issues

Rivers have always been very important to life in Africa. The continent's big rivers such as the Nile, Niger, and Congo are used to transport goods by boat. They are also a major source of water for farming and drinking. But while Africa has about 20% of the world's land area, it has less than 10% of the world's river water. Different areas of Africa have access to different amounts of water. This has a huge impact on the way people live and work.

Egypt is home to the Nile River, the longest river in the world. Egypt gets most of its water from the Nile River. Built across the Nile in southern Egypt, the Aswan High Dam stores water that is used to irrigate Egypt's farmland. This process causes environmental problems, however. Before the dam was built, the Nile used to flood each summer. The floodwaters carried nutrients that made the soil more fertile. Since the Aswan Dam now controls the flow of the Nile, the river no longer floods. The silt that once fertilized the land is now trapped behind the dam. Farmers depend on chemical fertilizers, which end up in the Nile River, polluting the water. Egypt's population growth has also led to heavy pollution of the Nile.

Pollution is a threat to agriculture, public health, and native plants and animals. The government of Egypt has passed laws designed to limit pollution. Other African nations have also passed laws that protect the environment.

Aswan High Dam

Many parts of Africa suffer from the lack of water. It is estimated that more than 300 million people in Africa lack access to clean drinking water. Most of these people live in rural areas. In many Sub-Saharan countries, people have to walk 30 minutes or more to the nearest source of water. The lack of clean water is a major cause of deadly diseases that affect millions of people each year.

Loss of Forests

Another major challenge to Africa's environment is **deforestation**, or the loss of forest land. Deforestation is the result of cutting down too many trees. People clear trees to use as fuel and to free up land for farming.

Africa has the highest rates of deforestation of any continent—more than twice as high as the world average. Nearly 10 million acres of forest are cleared each year. That is an area larger than the state of Maryland. The problem is most serious in central Africa, which has vast areas of tropical rainforest. Deforestation leads to other problems, such as the decline of soil quality. The roots of trees hold soil in place. When trees are cleared, soil can blow away in the wind. As a result, deforested land does not usually remain fertile for more than a few years. Forests are also home to many native species. The loss of these trees can lead to dangerous flash floods and the extinction of species.

Many African governments are working to reverse the damage. The government of South Africa, for example, has passed laws designed to protect the nation's remaining forests. Many trees have been planted in an effort to restore forests. **Reforestation** helps prevent soil erosion. South Africa has created many national parks. These parks help protect the natural environment, including animal and plant species.

Desertification

The loss of forests can contribute to another serious environmental problem, known as desertification. **Desertification** is the transformation of usable land into desert. When trees are cleared from an area, fertile soil can be blown away by wind. Dry, infertile dirt is left behind. The overgrazing of land can have the same effect. If animals eat all the grass and plants from an area, there is nothing to hold the soil in place.

Africa is more affected by desertification than any other continent. Desertification affects many countries in the Sahel, where the soil is relatively dry to begin with. The nation of Sudan is dry in the north and wet in the south. Water in the southern part of Sudan is supplied by the Nile River system. Sudan uses irrigation to supply water to farmlands. But drought and over-farming threaten Sudan's water resources. Desertification turns much of Sudan's farmland into unusable desert.

A Sudan oasis

The country of Mali suffers from severe **drought**, which is the absence of rainfall. The drought in Mali has led to desertification. Desertification can be caused by a number of factors. Mali's lack of fresh, clean water is very dangerous. Much of Mali's population is at risk for disease. The combination of drought and desertification is also dangerous to native animal species. Many species are near extinction.

Mali has created national parks. These natural areas are now protected by the government. In addition, Mali has also passed laws that protect the environment. These laws help stop desertification, protect endangered species, and increase biodiversity.

Oil and the Environment

Many African nations, such as Chad, are rich in oil. But getting oil out of the ground can be dangerous to the environment. Oil spills can kill native animal species. Accidents can also pollute water supplies. The people of Chad are concerned about oil spills. Chad's economy could be improved by using better and safer oil production technology. The government will need to balance the threats and the benefits of oil production to benefit their economy and to help their environment.

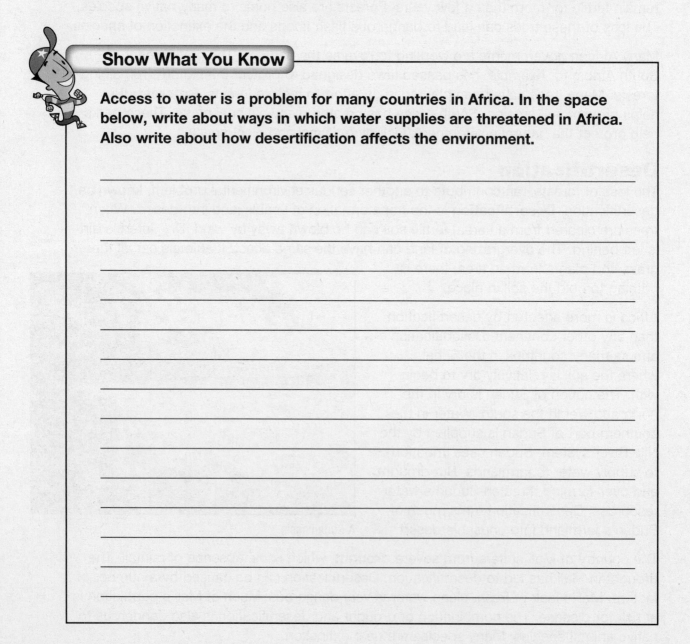

Show What You Know

Access to water is a problem for many countries in Africa. In the space below, write about ways in which water supplies are threatened in Africa. Also write about how desertification affects the environment.

Lesson Practice

Thinking It Through

1. Sudan's main source of water is

   A. the Red Sea.

   B. Lake Victoria.

   C. the Nile River.

   D. the Atlantic Ocean.

Sudan uses water from an important source. Its main source of water is also known as the longest river in the world.

2. What is one effect the Aswan High Dam has on the Nile River today?

   A. The Nile River is free from pollution.

   B. The Aswan High Dam slows the flow of the Nile River.

   C. Farmers use fewer chemical fertilizers.

   D. The Nile River floods more often than in the past.

   HINT *The Aswan High Dam was built to control the Nile River.*

3. The economy of Chad could MOST easily be improved by

   A. oil production.

   B. deforestation.

   C. the technology industry.

   D. desertification.

4. Which statement about deforestation is true?

   A. Deforestation is good for the soil.

   B. Deforestation cannot be reversed.

   C. Deforestation is helpful to native animal species.

   D. Deforestation can cause desertification.

10 Cultural Features of Africa

 SS7G4.a–b

Religions, Customs, and Traditions

Africa is made up of 54 different countries and many ethnic groups. An ethnic group is a cultural community of people with common ancestry, often sharing common religion, language, and traditions. A group's customs and traditions often come from religion, from where the group lives, or from the demands of daily life. For example, a nomadic Bedouin tribe must have customs that can be practiced while traveling.

There are also many different religious groups in Africa. Members of a religious group share the same religion. People from many different ethnic groups can be part of the same religious group. For example, most Africans today are either Muslim or Christian. However, traditional religions and customs still play a role in African culture.

Arab Diversity

The term **Arab** refers to a mixed ethnic group made up of people who speak the Arabic language. Arabs mostly live in North Africa and Southwest Asia. Some Jews, Kurds, Berbers, Copts, and Druze speak Arabic, but are not usually considered Arab. The term "Arab" includes Arabic-speaking Christians in Syria, Lebanon, Israel, and Jordan. Overall, Arabs are divided into two groups—nomadic Bedouins and settled Arabs.

The **Bedouin** are made up of several nomadic tribes who live in the deserts of Arabia, the Negev, and the Sinai. **Nomadic people** move from one place to another in search of food and water for themselves and their herds. An oasis can only support a group for a short time, and so the Bedouin people move on frequently. Leaving an oasis gives it a chance to replenish. The Bedouin religion is a combination of polytheism (a belief in many gods), Judaism, and Christianity.

The Bantu

The **Bantu** originally came from southeastern Nigeria, near the Benue-Cross Rivers that spread east and south near Zambia, in Central Africa. Around 1000 CE, the Bantu reached present-day Zimbabwe and South Africa. Here, the Bantu established the Munhumutapa Empire. This new empire controlled trading routes from South Africa to the area north of the Zambezi River. The Bantu traded many natural resources: gold, copper, precious stones, animal hides, ivory, and metal goods. They traded with Arab traders from the Swahili coast, as well as others. The empire collapsed in the early 16th century, after it used up all its resources.

Ashanti People

The **Ashanti** people live in central Ghana. The family, especially the mother's family, is most important to the Ashanti. They believe that children inherit their spirits from their father and their flesh and blood from their mother. The mystical Golden Stool has been the center of Ashanti spiritual practice since the late 17th century. It is said to have arrived on Earth by floating down from the heavens. The Ashanti people believe the strength of their nation depends on the safety of this stool. It represents the unity of the Ashanti and the power of their chiefs. The Ashanti honor kings after death, in a ceremony in which a stool is blackened.

Ashanti people

Swahili and Other Groups

The **Swahili** people live on the East African coast from southern Somalia to northern Mozambique. The Swahili people practice a strict form of Islam. In addition to Islamic beliefs, the Swahili believe in spirits, or djinns. Swahili Muslims use trances to speak to djinns. Men wear amulets around their necks that contain verses from the Qur'an, which they believe will protect them. Only teachers of Islam and prophets are permitted to become spiritual healers.

The Khoikhoi and San groups were the first people in present-day South Africa. For thousands of years they were hunter-gatherers. Around 400 CE, the Bantu began to push the Khoikhoi and San out of their lands. The Bantu were farmers and wanted the land. Both groups were pushed into the desert. The San believe that farming goes against the world order created by God. The San continued to hunt and gather in the Kalahari Desert. The Khoikhoi began to herd sheep. Some Khoikhoi settled in rich pastures and others nomadically moved with the herds.

There are several different San peoples, and they speak a variety of click languages. These languages include several different "click" sounds. San peoples have complex traditions of storytelling. Dance is also central in all San groups as a ritual that heals the community. Ritual dances are a community activity that transforms spiritual power and energy into medicine. Everyone who dances is healed by this energy, the San believe. Many San go into a trance as they gather the power of the dance. Dancing is used to heal both physical and mental illnesses.

Art and Music from Africa

The dance and music of Africa has many distinct styles and uses unique instruments. Sub-Saharan African music and dance is different from the music and dance of the Arab cultures of North Africa, or the Western settler populations of southern Africa. Many of the Sub-Saharan traditions are maintained by oral tradition. Song is viewed as a mode of communication. Several important writers have come from Africa. Since 1986, three writers from Africa have won the Nobel Prize in literature: Wole Soyinka of Nigeria, Naguib Mahfouz of Egypt, and Nadine Gordimer of South Africa.

Show What You Know

Choose one ethnic group mentioned in this lesson. In the space below, write about their cultural characteristics as compared to another group.

_____

_____

_____

_____

_____

_____

_____

_____

_____

_____

_____

_____

_____

_____

_____

_____

_____

_____

Lesson Practice

Circle the letter of the best answer for each item.

Thinking It Through

1. How did the Bantu expansion influence customs of the Khoikhoi?

   A. The Bantu brought gold for jewelry.

   B. The Khoikhoi began to herd sheep.

   C. The Khoikhoi and San converted to Islam.

   D. The Bantu taught the Khoikhoi and San to be farmers.

   The Bantu were farmers and sought new land. As they moved south, they pushed the Khoikhoi and the San from their usual land. Since they were pushed from their land, the Khoikhoi and the San had to learn new methods of survival.

2. The Ashanti believe the strength of their nation is dependent on

   A. the Golden Stool.

   B. the Silver Stool.

   C. the Golden Cross.

   D. the Silver Cross.

   HINT *It is said this floated down from the heavens.*

3. MOST Africans today are

   A. Arab.

   B. Ashanti.

   C. nomadic.

   D. Muslim or Christian.

4. Bedouin people move from one oasis to another to

   A. search for gold.

   B. search for food and water.

   C. bring messages to the next town.

   D. trade goods and animals.

11 African Health Issues

SS7CG3.a–b, SS7G4.c

Africa is a large continent with many countries and nearly one billion people. It is also the poorest continent in the world. There is widespread poverty throughout Africa. Many health problems are caused or made worse by poverty. Poverty creates poor living conditions, such as lack of clean water or food. People living in poor conditions often get sick. They may live in crowded areas that are dirty. They may not have doctors or medicine. People living in poverty may not have the education to know how to stop the spread of disease.

Famine in Africa

Famine occurs when a region does not have enough food for a long period of time. People who are starving can die from malnutrition. Famines are both human-made and natural. Drought, or lack of rain, makes food scarce because crops die. Human forces, like wars, can also cause food shortages. People in a region can be without food because its cost is too high. All of these factors have led to famines in Africa.

Famines in Africa today are mainly the result of poor food distribution and poverty. There is enough food on Earth for everyone to eat well. However, many people live where they cannot grow food. People also live where food cannot be easily transported.

The risk of famine is highest in Sub-Saharan Africa. Today, Niger, southern Sudan, Somalia, and Zimbabwe are areas with emergency famine status. Africa's greatest humanitarian crisis is in Darfur, in western Sudan. A humanitarian crisis is a situation in which many human lives are at risk in a region.

Malaria in Africa

Malaria is a tropical disease spread by mosquitoes. Each year, more than one million people die from malaria. Children in Sub-Saharan Africa are most at risk of death from the disease. For instance, malaria is the leading cause of death in children under five in Uganda. There is no vaccine against malaria. However, there are ways to reduce the spread of the disease. Insecticides and mosquito nets can drastically lower the number of infections. Antimalarial drugs can also help, but they are very expensive.

HIV and AIDS in Africa

The spread of **acquired immunodeficiency syndrome (AIDS)** due to infection by the **human immunodeficiency virus (HIV)** is the most severe health crisis in the world. It is considered a **pandemic**, a widespread epidemic. HIV/AIDS attacks and destroys the body's power to fight illness. HIV/AIDS is spread through bodily fluids like blood, semen, and breast milk. Africa has the highest rates of HIV infection in the world. Seventeen million people have died from AIDS on the continent. Over two-thirds of all HIV infections in the world are in Africa.

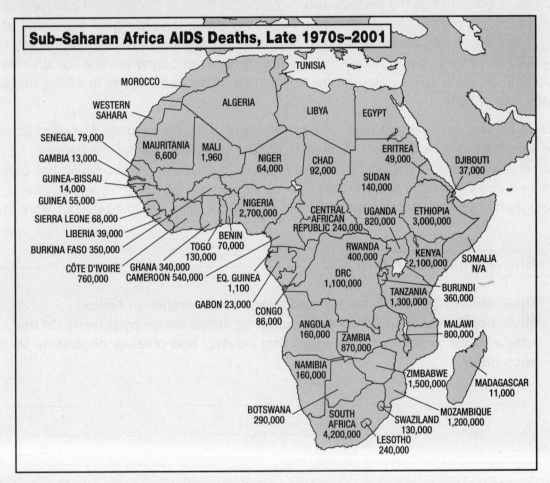

Sub-Saharan Africa AIDS Deaths, Late 1970s–2001

AIDS/HIV is a major threat to the people of Africa. The spread of AIDS lowers the life expectancy of entire populations. Life expectancy is a measure of how long people can expect to live. Over 12 million African children have been orphaned by AIDS. There are drugs that slow down the progression of HIV infection to AIDS. However, there is no cure for AIDS. Education and prevention are the most important tools for fighting AIDS. Africa needs more money to pay for education and prevention programs.

Famine and health issues in Africa are made worse by unstable politics. In turn, unstable politics contribute to poverty. High death rates due to health crises weaken economies. In this way, the issues of health, economics, and politics are intertwined.

Education and Literacy

African leaders agree that a quality education for all children will be a key to improving living conditions. Factors such as poverty and war, however, can limit children's access to education.

In Kenya, the government has worked hard to make free public schools available to all its citizens. While a lack of money has limited Kenya's success, the country's education system has improved greatly since Kenya achieved independence. One important measure of education is the **literacy rate**—the percentage of people who can read and write. Literacy gives people access to better jobs and can lead to higher standards of living. More developed countries tend to have a higher literacy rate. Kenya's literacy rate is over 80%, which is higher than most other Sub-Saharan countries. The literacy rate in Africa as a whole is 50%. South Africa, the most developed country in Africa, has a literacy rate of 86%.

Sudan's literacy rate is about 60%. The government of Sudan requires that all children from ages 6 to 13 attend school. Access to school varies throughout the country, however. Most schools are located in urban areas. In southern Sudan, which has been devastated by civil war, many children have no access to schools. Fewer girls attend school than boys. The literacy rate in Sudan is 70% for men, but just 50% for women.

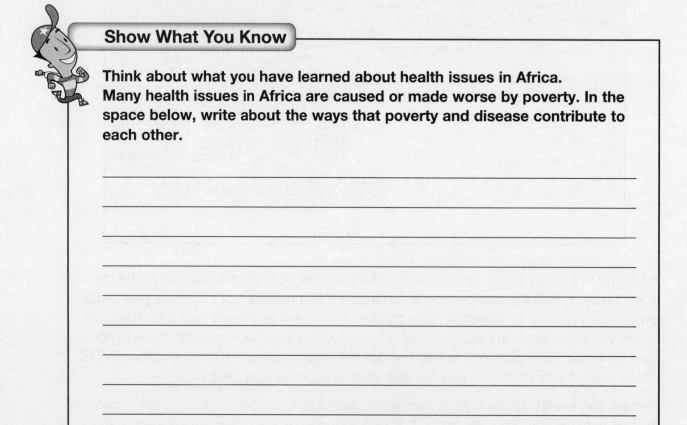

Show What You Know

Think about what you have learned about health issues in Africa. Many health issues in Africa are caused or made worse by poverty. In the space below, write about the ways that poverty and disease contribute to each other.

_____

_____

_____

_____

_____

_____

_____

_____

_____

_____

Lesson Practice

DIRECTIONS
Circle the letter of the best answer for each item.

Thinking It Through

1. How is malaria spread?

   A. by overfarming

   B. by dirty water

   C. by sharing combs

   D. by mosquitoes

   Malaria occurs in tropical climates where there are mosquitoes. When people cannot afford mosquito netting, malaria spreads more quickly.

2. What is NOT a cause of food shortages?

   A. lack of food on the planet

   B. wars

   C. droughts

   D. poor food distribution

   HINT *There is more than enough food to feed everyone on Earth.*

3. What is the name of the virus that causes AIDS?

   A. malaria

   B. malnutrition

   C. HIV

   D. WHO

4. Which of the following strategies would help in preventing the spread of HIV/AIDS in Africa?

   A. more tourism

   B. education and prevention

   C. fewer children

   D. fewer pets

12 African Governments

SS7CG2.a

Modern governments in Africa differ from one another. The governments of Kenya, South Africa, and Sudan, for instance, share some common traits. At the same time, they operate much differently from one another. One major difference is the role of citizens. Kenya and South Africa have democratic governments in which citizens choose their leaders in elections. In contrast, Sudan has had an authoritarian government for many years.

Kenya

In 1963, Kenya declared its independence from England. Kenya is a **republic**—a system in which citizens elect leaders to represent them. Until 1991, by law Kenya had only one political party. In 1992, Kenya held its first presidential election that included more than one candidate running for office. The executive branch, which includes the office of president, is the strongest branch of Kenyan government. The president serves a five-year term with a two-term limit and acts as head of state and head of government. The president appoints a cabinet of ministers and a vice president.

Kenya's legislature, or parliament, is a one-chamber body called the National Assembly, or Bunge. The president must approve any law passed by the National Assembly. Citizens of Kenya elect the majority of members of the National Assembly. Other members are appointed. All Kenyan citizens 18 or older are able to vote for the president and members of the National Assembly.

South Africa

Since the end of apartheid, South Africa has also been a democratic country. South Africa's new constitution was ratified in 1996. The constitution splits power between the executive and legislative branch, and contains a bill of rights for all South Africans. All citizens 18 and over have the right to vote.

Nelson Mandela was elected president of South Africa in 1994, winning the first election that was held after the adoption of universal suffrage.

The legislative branch of South Africa has two houses, the National Assembly and the National Council of Provinces. The National Assembly has 400 members elected by South African citizens for five-year terms. The National Council of Provinces has ten members from each province elected by provincial legislatures. The president is elected for a five-year term by the majority party in the National Assembly. The president appoints a deputy president and cabinet from members of the National Assembly.

Sudan

Unlike Kenya and South Africa, the citizens of Sudan have had little role in choosing their government in recent decades. In 1989, an army officer named Omar al-Bashir led a military coup, or takeover, in Sudan. The military seized complete control of the government and banned all political parties. Though he called himself president, Bashir ruled as a military dictator. He controlled the army and named governors for Sudan's 26 states.

In 2005, leaders from the various regions of Sudan agreed to a new constitution. Bashir stayed on as president, but political parties were legalized and elections planned. Though the future remains uncertain, the people may have the chance to elect a new government in 2010.

Morocco

Morocco has yet another form of government. It is a constitutional monarchy. A **constitutional monarchy** is one in which the head of state is a king or queen and in which the supreme law of the land is written down in a constitution. Morocco's monarch must be male, according to the constitution. He is the head of state and commander-in-chief of the armed forces of Morocco. The monarch appoints a prime minister and cabinet. He also has limited power over decisions of the legislature.

Morocco's constitutional monarchy has aspects that are similar to a representative democracy. In a **representative democracy**, the people elect representatives who act on their behalf in government. The Moroccan legislature consists of the House of Representatives and the House of Advisors. The House of Representatives has 325 members and the House of Advisors has 270. Representatives are elected through popular elections for five-year terms. Advisors are elected by various social organizations, and 30 seats are reserved for women.

Libya

The government of Libya is a *jamahiriya*, or "state of the masses." The government's structure is based on the political theory of Muammar al-Qaddafi. Qaddafi came to power in a 1969 military coup and is recognized as the head of state of Libya. According to Qaddafi, the government's power rests with the legislature.

The legislature of Libya is known as the General People's Congress, or GPC. However, Qaddafi retains power and influence over the government. Because of this, the government can be considered a military dictatorship. Members of the GPC are elected by local governments, or Basic People's Congresses (BPCs). There are 25 municipalities, divided into about 1,500 BPC. Every citizen belongs to a BPC.

Civil War and Conflict in Africa

Africa is the most politically unstable continent in the world. Limited natural resources, ethnic differences, and weak governments cause much conflict. For example, one of the more serious armed conflicts in the region is in the Democratic Republic of Congo (DRC). There are 200 ethnic groups with distinct languages in the country. These groups are often engaged in wars with one another. A war involving nine African nations raged from 1998 to 2002 in the DRC. Sparked by the fall of the state of Zaire, fighters waged war for control of the country's rich supplies of minerals, diamonds, and timber. The war directly affected the lives of 50 million Congolese. Almost four million people died in the DRC, mostly due to starvation and disease as a result of the conflict. Millions have become displaced within the country.

In 2002, a truce was declared, but many armed groups have not yet disarmed. In the eastern part of the DRC, armed groups funded by the neighboring country of Uganda were violent until 2004. Elections have been held in the DRC every year since 2006. In May 2009, further efforts were made to resolve the conflict in the east.

Show What You Know

There are 200 different languages spoken in Africa today. Write about what you think life would be like if people spoke 200 different languages in Georgia. Also write about how cultural diversity affects the government.

Lesson Practice

DIRECTIONS
Circle the letter of the best answer for each item.

Thinking It Through

1. Why is Kenya considered a republic?

   A. The citizens are not allowed to vote for president.

   B. The legislature has only one chamber.

   C. The leader of the country is a king.

   D. The citizens elect leaders to represent them.

   In Kenya, the citizens are allowed to vote. They vote for the president and members of the National Assembly. The country is not ruled by a monarch.

2. In which country is power split between the executive and legislative branches of government?

   A. Kenya

   B. South Africa

   C. Sudan

   D. Libya

   HINT *The country has a constitution that contains a bill of rights.*

3. Which of these countries is ruled by a dictator?

   A. Morocco

   B. South Africa

   C. Sudan

   D. Kenya

4. What are the two houses of the South African legislature?

   A. Parliament and the National Assembly

   B. The National Assembly and the National Council of Provinces

   C. The National Council of Provinces and the King's Council

   D. The King's Council and the National Assembly

13 African Trade

 SS7E2.a–b

Benefits of Trade

International trade has important benefits for both buyers and sellers in Africa. When two countries trade, people in both countries gain access to goods and services they want to use. They also gain a place to sell the goods they produce and the services they provide.

As in other parts of the world, many African nations specialize in producing certain kinds of goods or services. Africa is a continent rich in minerals. Many African countries specialize in products based on the nonrenewable natural resources found in that country. The Central African Republic, for example, earns almost half of all its export earnings from the sale of diamonds.

Algeria specializes in the production of oil and gas. In fact, these products account for more than 97% of Algeria's exports. The money earned is then used to buy products Algerians want, such as machinery and electronic goods. Due to its huge oil and gas earnings, Algeria has a large **trade surplus**. This means the value of its exports is greater than the value of its imports. Countries that import more than they export have a **trade deficit**.

Trade Barriers

Governments sometimes limit what can be traded to their people and with whom their people can trade. These types of limits are trade barriers. A country might impose a tariff, or a tax on imports, to help a certain industry. Suppose a country imposes a tariff on paper, for example. Imported paper would then become more expensive in that country. This might encourage people to buy paper made within the country.

Import quotas are another form of trade barrier. Quotas limit the number of goods that can be imported from a certain country. A quota has a similar effect to a tariff, because it makes a certain item harder to get, and thus, more expensive.

An embargo, or a ban on trade with a certain country, is normally put in place for political reasons. During the time of apartheid in South Africa, many other African nations refused to trade with South Africa. More recently, the United States and other countries placed a weapons embargo on Sudan. U.S. leaders hoped the refusal to sell arms to Sudan's dictatorship would help lead to change in the country.

Trade Agreements

Many African countries are working to remove trade barriers, with the hope that increased trade will benefit their economies. One of the goals of the African Union (AU) is to remove trade barriers between African nations.

Other regional agreements also remove trade barriers in Africa. Nine South African countries came together in 1980 to form a treaty. The **Southern African Development Community (SADC)** assists in making government and monetary policies for its member countries. Five new countries have joined since 1980. The group promotes economic development. Many African states are trying to lower their poverty rates. By working together, these countries hope to build southern Africa financially.

Sixteen West African countries made a pact in 1975. They signed a treaty hoping to promote strength in the region. The **Economic Community of West African States (ECOWAS)** was formed in order to join together and develop the economies of member states. Their goal is to raise the standard of living and stability of the region.

Exchanging Currencies

Most of the countries of Africa use different currencies. Some examples of African money are the Egyptian pound, the South African rand, the Nigerian naira, and Chad's franc. As part of the goal of linking their economies and removing barriers to trade, some countries have agreed to use the same currency. Fourteen former French colonies in western and central Africa all use a currency called the CFA franc.

In order for countries with different currencies to buy and sell each other's goods, an exchange rate is necessary. The exchange rate is the current value of one country's currency compared to another country's currency. For example, at the end of 2009, one U.S. dollar was worth about 7.5 South African rand. Exchange rates change daily. The changes are based on factors like government stability and the strength of a country's economy.

African countries use many different currencies.

Show What You Know

What are some reasons African countries are trying to unite their economies? Write your response below.

_____

_____

_____

_____

_____

_____

_____

_____

_____

_____

_____

_____

_____

_____

_____

_____

_____

_____

_____

_____

_____

_____

_____

_____

_____

Lesson Practice

DIRECTIONS
Circle the letter of the best answer for each item.

Thinking It Through

1. The U.S. refusal to sell weapons to Sudan is an example of

   A. a quota.

   B. a tariff.

   C. an embargo.

   D. a sale.

A quota is a limit on the amount of a good that can be imported. A sale is when a good or service is exchanged for money. A tariff is a tax on imported goods.

2. Which of the following is a main goal of the African Union?

   A. end apartheid

   B. reduce environmental laws

   C. eliminate trade barriers

   D. increase tariffs on farm products

HINT *AU members believe that more trade can help Africa's economies grow.*

3. Algeria makes nearly all of its export earnings from oil and gas. This is an example of

   A. specialization.

   B. a trade barrier.

   C. currency integration.

   D. a quota.

4. What is one important benefit of the currency exchange rate?

   A. It makes international trade possible.

   B. It acts as a trade barrier.

   C. It eliminates embargoes between countries.

   D. It stays the same from day to day.

14 African Economies

 SS7E1.c, SS7E3.a–d

Comparing Economies: Nigeria and South Africa

Nigeria and South Africa have two of the largest economies in Africa. The most common way to measure the size of a national economy is by gross domestic product, or GDP. **Gross domestic product** is the total value of all the goods and services produced by a country each year. Nigeria has the third-largest GDP, at about $335 billion. South Africa's GDP of $500 billion is the highest in Africa.

While Nigeria and South Africa have large economies, there are important differences between the countries. Since the 1960s, Nigeria's economy has become heavily based on the production and sale of oil. In fact, about 80% of Nigeria's entire government budget comes from oil profits. Oil brings billions of dollars into Nigeria, but it also creates problems. The price of oil is highly volatile, meaning it can rise and fall rapidly. When the price falls, the entire economy suffers.

South Africa's economy was hurt by economic sanctions during the apartheid era. The economy began to recover in the mid-1990s, after the end of apartheid. South Africa's economy is more **diversified** than Nigeria's. This means that a larger number of different industries contribute to the nation's economy. South Africa is a major producer of agricultural goods and motor vehicles. Valuable metals such as gold and platinum are also major exports.

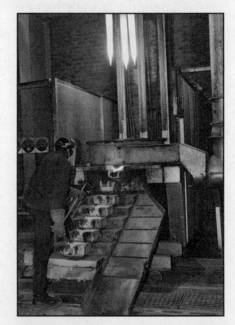

Many South Africans work in the gold mining industry.

Both Nigeria and South Africa have mixed economies, with elements of the free market system mixed with some government control. In both countries, the government used to play a much larger role in deciding what was produced and how. In recent years, both countries have moved away from command economies. In South Africa, the government has sold previously government-owned industries, such as steel and railroads. But it retains control of some important industries, like the country's main electric utility. Similarly, the Nigerian government has sold several oil and chemical companies that were once owned by the government.

Human Capital and Capital Resources

Many factors affect a country's gross domestic product. For example, human capital is needed to make any industry work well. **Human capital** is the value of people's work. A skilled worker is valuable to businesses and the nation.

Investing in human capital is important to financial growth. For example, machines on a farm must be maintained. Machines need things like fuel and regular repair. Providing training, education, and medicine to workers is just as important. It helps the business make money if its workers are skilled and healthy.

Any goods that are used to produce other goods are **capital goods**. Capital goods include machinery or even factories. Investment in capital goods is another key to strong economic growth. By investing in new computers and technology, a factory may be able to produce goods more quickly and at lower costs.

Entrepreneurs are also very important to strong economic growth. An **entrepreneur** is a person who takes the risk of organizing and running a new business. Entrepreneurs help the economy, because growing companies create new jobs for people, and produce goods and services that contribute to the national economy.

Natural Resources and Economies

Africa is a continent rich in nonrenewable natural resources, including large amounts of oil and gas, useful metals such as iron, chromium, and lead, and valuable minerals including gold, rubies, and diamonds. Distribution of these resources has had a large impact on economic development in Africa.

South Africa is home to huge deposits of gold—about half the entire world's total. Gold can also be found in Kenya and Egypt. The world's largest diamond deposits are also found in South Africa. The mining of these resources has been a major industry in South Africa for many years. Diamonds are a major source of income in Congo. Kenya also has deposits of rubies and topazes, as well as soda ash, which is used in glassmaking.

Oil reserves have been found in northern African nations, including Nigeria, Sudan, and Egypt. In Nigeria, the vast reserves of crude oil have not been fully exploited due to economic instability and a large national debt. The ongoing civil war in Sudan makes it difficult for the government to exploit the oil reserves. Egypt's oil reserves are not as vast as those of the other countries, but Egypt does have an abundance of natural gas.

Many valuable uranium mines are located in southern Africa and in Egypt. One pound of uranium can release as much energy as three million pounds of coal. This makes uranium useful as fuel for nuclear reactors, which produce electricity. It can also be used to make atomic bombs. This makes it an extremely dangerous resource, as well as a valuable resource. Egypt also has deposits of iron ore and chromium.

All of these resources are important to the countries where they are found. At the same time, African leaders realize the danger of being too dependent on the sale of just one or two resources.

Show What You Know

Complete the chart below by listing one valuable natural resource found in each of the countries listed.

Country	One important resource
Congo	
Egypt	
Kenya	
Nigeria	
South Africa	
Sudan	

Lesson Practice

Thinking It Through

1. Today Nigeria and South Africa BOTH have

   A. pure market economies.

   B. command economies.

   C. mixed economies.

   D. traditional economies.

   There are very few economies in the world today that are controlled by the government. Most economies today have some government and some market control.

2. New technology, factories, and machinery are all

   A. human capital.

   B. natural resources.

   C. capital goods.

   D. economic systems.

   HINT *Capital goods are goods that must be purchased in order to make other goods.*

3. An entrepreneur is

   A. a head of state in control of resources.

   B. a dictator.

   C. a person in charge of international trade.

   D. a person who takes risks by starting a new business.

4. The total value of all the goods and services produced by a country each year is known as the country's

   A. gross domestic product.

   B. national debt.

   C. trade balance.

   D. total export earnings.

2 Review

Choose the best answer for each question. Fill in the circle of the spaces provided on your answer sheet.

1. Which of the following factors has worsened the AIDS pandemic in Africa?

   A. formation of the African Union

   B. international aid

   C. unstable governments

   D. trade agreements

2. All of the following were negative impacts of Europe's partitioning of Africa EXCEPT

   A. civil wars.

   B. riots and protests.

   C. separation of tribes.

   D. end of the slave trade.

3. What is the purpose of a currency exchange rate?

   A. It increases the gross domestic product for one country while lowering it for another.

   B. It acts as a barrier between countries that want to trade.

   C. It enables trade between countries that have different currencies.

   D. It puts an end to trade barriers.

4. From which country did Kenya struggle for independence?

   A. Portugal

   B. Britain

   C France

   D. Belgium

5. The world's largest desert, located in northern Africa, is called the

    A. White.

    B. Sahara.

    C. Sahel.

    D. Kalahari.

6. The first South African president chosen in an election open to voters of all races was

    A. Nelson Mandela.

    B. Kwame Nkrumah.

    C. Jomo Kenyatta.

    D. King Leopold III.

7. One important cause of water pollution in Egypt is

    A. oil spills in the Mediterranean.

    B. chemical fertilizers that flow into the Nile River.

    C. gold mining waste in South Africa.

    D. the building of dams on the Congo River.

8. The economy of Nigeria is heavily dependent on the sale of

    A. gold.

    B. diamonds.

    C. uranium.

    D. oil.

Use the map below to answer questions 9 and 10.

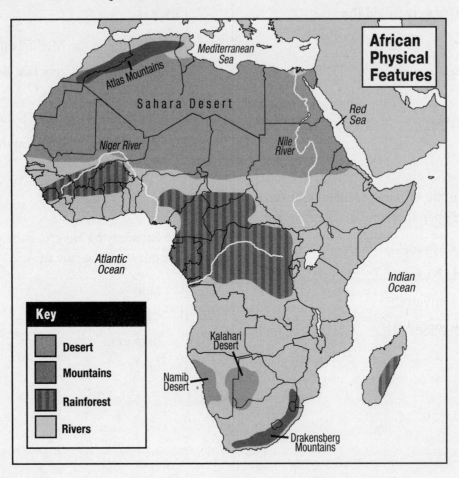

9. The Kalahari Desert extends into the northern part of

   A. Sudan.

   B. Nigeria.

   C. Kenya.

   D. South Africa.

10. The Sahara Desert covers the northern half of which of the following countries?

   A. Congo

   B. Kenya

   C. South Africa

   D. Sudan

11. What is the effect of a country investing in capital goods such as factories, machineries, and technology?

    A. It encourages more people to become entrepreneurs.

    B. It helps remove trade barriers.

    C. It helps lower the currency exchange rate.

    D. It helps the gross domestic product grow.

12. How does literacy affect people's standard of living?

    A. Literacy often leads to a higher standard of living.

    B. Literacy rates have little impact on standards of living.

    C. Low literacy rates can lead to better jobs.

    D. Low literacy rates make countries well developed.

13. During the years of apartheid, some African nations refused to buy products from South Africa. This was an example of

    A. an embargo.

    B. a quota.

    C. a tariff.

    D. a free trade agreement.

14. What impact does desertification have on Africa?

    A. More fertile soil is gained.

    B. Fresh water is preserved.

    C. New forests are planted.

    D. Valuable farmland is lost.

15. Why did European powers colonize Africa?

    A. They wanted to spread their languages.

    B. They wanted Africa's valuable natural resources.

    C. They wanted to spread Islam.

    D. They wanted to export natural resources to Africa.

16. One major impact of the Pan-African movement is that

    A. the problem of water pollution has been solved.

    B. African nations have united to form the African Union.

    C. many African nations are still colonies today.

    D. all African nations are now stable democracies.

Use the timeline below to answer question 17.

17. Which statement BEST represents the facts given in the timeline?

   A. The mid-20th century was a time of colonization of Africa.

   B. Europe was strengthening its power in Africa at this time.

   C. The mid-20th century was a time of nationalism in Africa.

   D. Drought was a major issue during the era.

18. All of the following are examples of entrepreneurs EXCEPT

   A. a new restaurant owner.

   B. a concert promoter.

   C. a military general.

   D. a child with a lemonade stand.

19. Who is Frederick Willem de Klerk?

   A. the leader of the African National Congress

   B. the first European to arrive in South Africa

   C. the first president elected by democratic election in South Africa

   D. the South African president who helped end apartheid

20. Sudan and Egypt's main source of water is

   A. the Red Sea.

   B. Lake Victoria.

   C. the Nile River.

   D. the Atlantic Ocean.

21. Education, training, and healthcare are all

    A. investments in human capital.

    B. natural resources.

    C. capital goods.

    D. entrepreneurs.

22. In terms of religious belief, MOST Africans today

    A. follow faiths of nomadic peoples.

    B. are either Muslim or Christian.

    C. are either Muslim or Buddhist.

    D. follow the beliefs of the Ashanti people.

23. Which of the following is NOT a true statement about ethnic groups?

    A. Ethnic groups are cultural communities.

    B. Members of an ethnic group often share traditions.

    C. Each ethnic group has its own religion.

    D. Members of an ethnic group often share a language.

24. One way African governments are working to reverse deforestation is by

    A. expanding desertification.

    B. protecting coastlines.

    C. planting trees.

    D. banning irrigation.

25. All of these countries are located south of the Sahara Desert EXCEPT

    A. Egypt.

    B. Zimbabwe.

    C. Tanzania.

    D. Kenya.

26. The government of Kenya could BEST be described as

A. a constitutional monarchy.

B. an absolute monarchy.

C. a dictatorship.

D. a republic.

27. Which of the following factors has limited access to schools for children in Sudan?

A. lack of schools in urban areas

B. laws requiring all children from ages 6 to 13 to attend school

C. higher government spending on education

D. civil war in southern Sudan

Use the list below to answer question 28.

- located in western Africa

- borders Atlantic Ocean

- has areas of tropical rainforest

28. This list describes

A. South Africa.

B. Kenya.

C. Egypt.

D. Nigeria.

29. Which group of people practice a strict form of Islam combined with traditional beliefs?

    A. Ashanti

    B. Swahili

    C. Khoikhoi

    D. Bantu

30. Based on gross domestic product, the country in Africa with the largest economy is

    A. South Africa.

    B. Egypt.

    C. Nigeria.

    D. Sierra Leone.

31. Following a military takeover of the government in 1989, Omar al-Bashir acted as the authoritarian ruler of

    A. Libya.

    B. Sudan.

    C. South Africa.

    D. Kenya.

32. What is one thing the nationalist movements of Nigeria and South Africa had in common?

    A. Both defeated Great Britain militarily.

    B. Apartheid was established in both countries.

    C. Both achieved independence without war.

    D. Both remain colonies of European powers.

33. When a country charges a tax on imported goods, this is known as

A. a tariff.

B. an embargo.

C. a quota.

D. a sanction.

34. As a result of the Berlin Conference in 1884 and 1885

A. most African nations were granted independence.

B. the Nile River was dammed to stop floods.

C. Africa gained new colonies overseas.

D. nearly all of Africa was divided among European powers.

35. Droughts are very dangerous for the people of the Sahel. One main reason is that

A. most people rely on farming.

B. thick rainforests cover the region.

C. oil is the major industry.

D. diamond mining employs most people.

36. The mountain range that extends across North Africa is called the

A. Andes Mountains.

B. Atlas Mountains.

C. Drakensberg Mountains.

D. Alps Mountains.

CHAPTER 3
Southwest Asia (Middle East)

15 Origins of Judaism, Christianity, and Islam

 SS7G8.c–d

Three of the world's major religions originated in Southwest Asia: Judaism, Christianity, and Islam. All are based on monotheism, a belief in one god. Each religion has a sacred text, or book, which is at the core of its faith. Each book is a collection of writings compiled over time. None was written by the central figure of the faith.

Origins of Judaism

Judaism is the oldest of the three religions. It began as a set of beliefs and laws practiced by ancient Hebrew people in Southwest Asia. They were the first people to believe in one god. Judaism's book is the Hebrew *Bible*. Jews believe that one day a human leader will come as a messenger of God and bring about a golden age. They call this leader the *messiah*. In Greek versions of the Bible, *messiah* is written as *christos*, "the anointed one."

The Bible names Abraham as the father of the Jews. There is no other evidence of his life. Scholars place Abraham as living sometime between 2000 and 1500 BCE. The Bible states that Abraham was born in Ur, in present-day Iraq. He later moved to Canaan, in present-day Israel. Jews believe Canaan is the Promised Land, which God promised to Abraham and his descendants.

It is said that Abraham's grandson Jacob had twelve sons. The twelve tribes of Israel began with Jacob's sons. Jacob was later called Israel, and his descendants are called Israelites.

According to the Bible, the First Temple for Jewish worship was built around 1000–900 BCE and destroyed by Babylonians in 586 BCE. The Jews were then sent out of Canaan, but returned after 50 years in exile. A diaspora occurs when a group of people leave their homeland and move to many different locations. All of the world's Jewish communities today that do not live in present-day Israel are part of the Jewish diaspora.

Jews worship in synagogues.

A new temple was finished 70 years later on the site of the First Temple, but was badly plundered by invading Romans in approximately 54 BCE. King Herod, a Jew, ruled Judea for the Romans. The second temple was rebuilt in 20 BCE. When Romans attacked Jerusalem again in 70 CE, they destroyed Herod's temple. Today, the single remaining temple wall, the Western Wall, is a place of prayer for Jewish pilgrims. Jews moved away from the land again, but returned in large numbers when the modern state of Israel was formed in the late 1940s.

The Western Wall

Origins of Christianity

In 30 CE, a Jew named Jesus began preaching new ideas about Judaism in Roman-controlled Judea. The later title of *Jesus Christ* given to Jesus is a reference to the belief by followers of **Christianity** that he is the Jewish messiah.

According to the Christian *New Testament*, Jesus preached to his fellow Jews. His idea was that the old laws of Judaism should be replaced by a simpler system based on love of one's fellow human beings. He became

Jesus and the disciples

popular. Jewish leaders did not want Jesus to threaten their power and asked the Romans to arrest him. The Romans found him guilty of speaking against Jewish laws and sentenced him to death by crucifixion, or by being hung on a cross. He died in 33 CE, after preaching for only three years.

Jesus had twelve close followers, or disciples. Interestingly, a man who had never met Jesus became the person to spread his message of love around the world. Paul of Tarsus had a vision of Jesus after the crucifixion that told him to teach Jesus's ideas to non-Jews. Paul traveled throughout the ancient world to build churches in Ephesus, Corinth, Rome, and other cities. The New Testament records Paul's journeys through a series of letters, or epistles, that he wrote.

The chapters of Romans, Corinthians, Ephesians, Galatians, and Thessalonians are all letters written by Paul to the people of new, non-Jewish churches established in these locations. Paul taught them how to live their lives in these letters.

By 100 CE, the growth of Christianity was left to a new generation of people who had never known Jesus and who did not know Jewish laws. Roman authorities fought the growth of Christianity. Christians were often arrested and killed. Most Christians practiced their religion in hiding, but their numbers continued to grow and the religion spread.

By the early 4th century, Christianity may have reached members of the Roman emperor's family. The Roman Emperor Constantine was not a Christian, but he had his soldiers fight an important battle in 313 CE with a Christian symbol on their shields. His army won the battle.

In the first 300 years after his death, many different ideas developed about how to follow Jesus's teachings. In 325 CE, Constantine called a meeting for all the Christian leaders to meet in Nicea. About 300 men attended the meeting to discuss how Christianity should be practiced. The council produced the Nicene Creed, the first attempt at a uniform statement of Christian doctrine. When the Christian leaders left this meeting, a new type of Christian church had been formed. This new church was said to be *Catholic*, which means "universal."

Christians worship in churches.

Origins of Islam

The prophet Muhammad was an Arab born in 570 CE, in Mecca, which is in present-day Saudi Arabia. He was a merchant known as "al-Amin," the trustworthy one. According to Islamic tradition, in 610 CE, while he was praying in a cave, he had a vision of the angel Gabriel, a figure in the Hebrew Bible. The angel gave him messages from God, called *Allah* in Arabic.

Muhammad spread the messages he received from Allah. He was forced to flee Mecca for Medina in 622 CE. This flight is known as the *Hijrah*. The Islamic calendar begins at this date. By the time he died in 632 CE, Islamic control of central Arabia was well underway.

Muslims worship in mosques.

After Muhammad's death in 632 CE, Muhammad's followers began fighting over his successor. Followers of **Islam** are called Muslims. Some followers believed leadership of the Islamic community should remain in the hands of Muhammad's family. They wanted Muhammad's son-in-law, Ali ibn Abi Talib, to become the new leader. This group became known as the Shi'as. Others disagreed, arguing that following Islamic law was more important than the specific leader of the community. They believed a new leader should be chosen, but that it was not essential that he come from Muhammad's family. This group became known as the Sunnis.

The disagreement between the Shi'a and the Sunni led to a permanent split in the Muslim community. Today, the Shi'a comprise 10%–15% of Islamic followers. Most Shi'a live in Iran, as well as southern Iraq and Lebanon. The Sunni comprise close to 90% of the Muslim population worldwide.

The Five Pillars of Islam is the term for the religion's five main beliefs. They are accepted by all Sunnis and Shi'as, but the Shi'as have added several other practices to form the Branches of Religion. The Five Pillars are:

> Believe in only one God and Muhammad is his messenger.
> Pray in the direction of Mecca five times a day.
> Donate money to the poor.
> Fast during the month of Ramadan.
> Make a journey, or hajj, to Mecca at least once.

Islam has other rules, including what Muslims are allowed to eat and drink.

An Islamic Golden Age lasted from 750 to 1400 CE. Advances in Islamic learning inspired the European Renaissance. The city of Mecca became a major economic center, helping Islam expand. Literacy was, for the first time, widespread among the populations of Southwest Asia.

In 1258, the Islamic city of Baghdad was attacked, conquered, and destroyed by the Mongols, a dynasty from central Asia. The Islamic Golden Age began to draw to a close.

It is a Muslim goal to travel to Mecca.

Show What You Know

Make a timeline for the development of Judaism, Christianity, and Islam. Be sure to include the dates found in this lesson. What can you conclude from your timeline about the development of these religions?

_____

_____

_____

_____

_____

_____

_____

_____

Lesson Practice

DIRECTIONS
Circle the letter of the best answer for each item.

Thinking It Through

1. Around 52 CE, Paul of Tarsus began to write letters. What was the purpose of these letters?

   A. to teach Muslims how to fight for Islam

   B. to teach Jews how to practice Judaism

   C. to teach non-Jewish churches how to practice Christianity

   D. to teach non-Jewish churches how to practice Judaism

   Another word for letter is epistle. Many people from such places as Rome, Corinth, Ephesus, and Galatia are familiar with Paul's epistles.

2. When Herod built a temple in Jerusalem, the city was part of the

   A. diaspora.

   B. British Empire.

   C. Ottoman Empire.

   D. Roman Empire.

   HINT *Herod was awarded the kingship of Judea by the Roman emperor.*

3. The Western Wall is an important part of Jewish tradition today for all of the following reasons EXCEPT

   A. it was once the western wall of Herod's temple.

   B. it is prayed at daily by Jewish pilgrims.

   C. it was the most important building in Mecca.

   D. it was built on the site of the First Temple.

4. Which helped the spread of Islam?

   A. the death of Paul of Tarsus

   B. the Council of Nicea

   C. the birth of Jacob

   D. the Arabic literacy rate

16 The Ottoman Empire

 SS7H2.a

The **Ottoman Empire** began in 1299, in Turkey, which is located in southwestern Asia. The empire grew and later included parts of Southwest Asia, Africa, and Europe.

The Turks had been ruled by the Byzantine Empire prior to 1299. By the 13th century, the Byzantine Empire was in decline. Osman was a Turkish warrior and a Muslim. He had many followers, called Ottomans. In 1299, Osman conquered the last of the Byzantine villages and the Ottoman Empire began. Osman was the first Ottoman sultan. A **sultan** is the ruler of a Muslim state.

Growth

The Ottoman Empire grew fast by taking over many regions. Soon it was one of the largest empires in the world. By 1451, the Ottomans ruled many cities in Southwest Asia and Europe. Ottoman sultans were great military leaders. In 1453, the Ottomans took Constantinople (later called Istanbul). Constantinople was the capital of the Ottoman Empire. It was one of the largest cities of the time. For years it had been a center for culture and learning, the seat of both the Roman Empire and the Byzantine Empire. It had great architecture and art.

The 16th century was the golden age of the Ottoman Empire. Selim I was sultan from 1512 to 1520. He took the empire farther south and east, to the present-day areas of Syria, Israel, and Egypt. He was also given the keys to Mecca.

Suleyman, the son of Selim I, ruled from 1520 to 1566. He expanded the empire to the west. He moved into Hungary and captured Belgrade and the island of Rhodes. He was known as Suleyman the Magnificent. He died in 1566, by which time he was the best-known Muslim leader in the world.

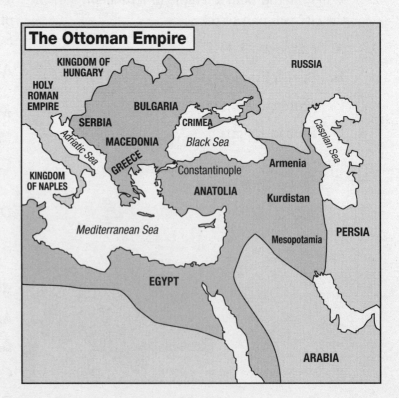

The Ottoman Empire

KINGDOM OF HUNGARY
HOLY ROMAN EMPIRE
RUSSIA
BULGARIA
SERBIA
CRIMEA
Adriatic Sea
MACEDONIA
Black Sea
Caspian Sea
GREECE
KINGDOM OF NAPLES
Constantinople
Armenia
ANATOLIA
Kurdistan
Mediterranean Sea
Mesopotamia
PERSIA
EGYPT
ARABIA

By 1500, the Ottoman Empire held the eastern Mediterranean, North Africa, and parts of Arabia. It controlled the trade of Southwest Asia and Europe's access to goods from the East.

Impact

All Ottoman rulers followed Islam. As the empire grew, Islamic culture spread. Many Muslims today still live in Eastern Europe, a remnant of Ottoman culture.

The Ottoman Empire controlled many trade routes. It had access to the Persian Gulf, the Black Sea, and the Mediterranean Sea. Europe and Asia were linked by Ottoman trade routes. This connection helped join these distant cultures.

Most countries of Western Europe treated the Ottoman Empire as a threat. European Christians feared the spread of Islam. Many European traders did not want to trade with the Ottomans because of this fear. All trade routes to the east were under Ottoman control. Western Europeans began to search for other ways to reach Asia. This search led to the age of exploration, during which the Americas were discovered and explored.

Decline and Partition

After Suleyman's death, the Ottoman Empire declined over the next 300 years. The empire gained and lost territory several times during that period. First, the empire lost parts of Europe. It was called the "Sick Man of Europe."

By the 20th century, the Ottoman Empire was weak. It sided with the Central powers in World War I, which fought against the Allied powers of England, France, Russia, and the United States. Ottoman troops won only one key battle in World War I, the Battle of Gallipoli.

The British took control of Jerusalem and Baghdad from the Ottomans. Arabia then rose up against Ottoman rule. By 1918, the Ottoman Empire had ended. The modern Turkish republic was declared on October 29, 1923. Today, Turkey is the largest Muslim country in Europe.

After World War I, the Treaty of Sèvres divided the land of the Ottoman Empire among Allied, or Western, powers. France gained control of Syria and Lebanon. The United Kingdom was granted Palestine and Iraq. This partitioning of Middle Eastern land led to years of regional conflict. Many people in these countries joined nationalist groups and began fighting for independence. In Syria, for example, armed rebels battled French forces. Syria declared its independence in 1936. The country officially became independent of France in 1946.

The UK also faced violent opposition in the lands it controlled. In Palestine, both Jews and Arabs fought the British for control of the territory. At the same time, Iraqi nationalists battled Britain for control of Iraq. Britain was convinced to leave Iraq, which became an independent country in 1932.

Show What You Know

Using a map, find the countries of the Ottoman Empire mentioned in this lesson. Choose two countries that were once a part of the Ottoman Empire. Using this lesson and others in this book, make a list of facts that you have learned about each country throughout history.

_____

_____

_____

_____

_____

_____

_____

_____

_____

_____

_____

_____

_____

_____

_____

_____

_____

_____

_____

_____

Lesson Practice

DIRECTIONS
Circle the letter of the best answer for each item.

Thinking It Through

1. What period is considered the golden age of the Ottoman Empire?

   A. the 13th century

   B. the 20th century

   C. the 15th century

   D. the 16th century

   During this time, the empire expanded the most quickly. It took over parts of Europe. Suleyman was a sultan of this era.

2. At the time of his death, which of these men was the MOST important Muslim leader in the world?

   A. Osman

   B. Suleyman

   C. Selim

   D. Napoleon

   HINT *He expanded the Ottoman Empire into Europe.*

3. The Ottoman Empire helped spread which religion?

   A. Judaism

   B. Hinduism

   C. Islam

   D. Christianity

4. What happened to the Ottoman Empire after World War I?

   A. It regained control of Southwest Asia.

   B. Much of its land was divided among Western powers.

   C. Most of its people converted to Islam.

   D. It gained control of North Africa.

17 The State of Israel

SS7H2.b

The modern state of Israel was established in 1948. Many beliefs and events led to its creation. One factor was the Jewish religious connection to the land. Israelite tribes are believed to have settled in Israel more than 3,200 years ago. According to the Bible, Jews built the First Temple in Jerusalem about 1000–900 BCE. In modern times, this ancient connection to the land inspired many Jews to dream of building their own homeland in Palestine.

The Zionist Movement

Another important event leading to the establishment of Israel was the rise of Zionism. **Zionism** is a Jewish movement that began in Europe in the late 19th century. Its goal was to establish a Jewish homeland in Palestine. Theodor Herzl started the movement and also led the first Zionist Congress in 1897. After World War I, the movement grew in popularity. In 1917, Britain issued the **Balfour Declaration**, which stated that Britain would work toward the establishment of a national home for the Jewish people in Palestine.

Many Arabs did not support Zionism. Nevertheless, the Jewish population in Palestine continued to grow. In just 30 years, from 1903 to 1933, the Jewish population grew from 25,000 to 238,000 as Jews moved to the region. By 1936, about one third of the total population of Palestine was made up of Jewish immigrants.

In 1937, the British created a plan to divide up the land between the Arabs and Jews, but both groups rejected it. The conflict between the Arabs and the Jews continued to get worse in the years leading up to World War II.

European Anti-Semitism

Events in Europe played a large role in the foundation of Israel. **Anti-Semitism** is hostility toward, or prejudice against, Jews or Judaism. In the late 19th and early 20th centuries, anti-Semitism began to spread throughout Europe. Events in Russia, Austria, and France fueled European anti-Semitism. In Russia, anti-Jewish mob attacks, called **pogroms**, began in 1881 and then spread to Central and Eastern Europe. Russians blamed Jews for the assassination of the tsar, the leader of Russia.

In 1894, a man named Alfred Dreyfus, who was the only Jewish member of the French army's general staff, was accused and convicted of spying for Germany. Ten years later, he was found innocent, but his original conviction sparked anti-Semitic riots in Paris. The crowds in the streets shouted "Death to the Jews." This was known as the **Dreyfus Affair**. The trial was closely followed by Americans.

In Austria in the late 1890s, politicians tried to keep additional Jews from moving into the Austro-Hungarian Empire. Leaders such as the mayor of Vienna encouraged anti-Semitic views and supported laws that were racist.

In each of these and many other cases, Jews were often irrationally blamed for events over which they had no control and in which they played no part. This type of misplaced blame without proof is a common feature of racist belief systems like anti-Semitism.

World War II

From the time Adolf Hitler became the chancellor of Germany in 1933, the treatment of Jews in Germany, and eventually most of continental Europe, grew worse. The policies of Hitler's Nazi Party slowly eroded the rights of Jews. The government declared that Jews were no longer German citizens and removed them from their jobs, businesses, schools, and homes. As Germany took over other European countries, including Poland, Czechoslovakia, the Netherlands, France, much of Russia, and Austria, Jews in those locations were treated similarly or worse. By the end of the war, Hitler's "final solution" to rid Earth of Jews resulted in the murder of six million Jews and the deaths of millions of other Europeans. This is known as the **Holocaust**. Jews who were able to flee Europe moved to Palestine during this time. The Holocaust ended with Germany's defeat in World War II in 1945.

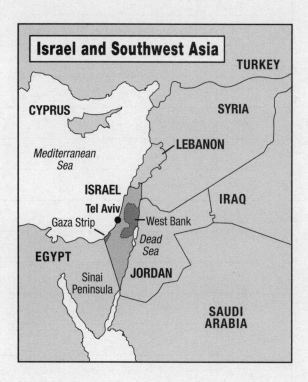

The Creation of Israel

After World War II and the Holocaust, many world leaders agreed that Jews needed to have a country of their own. In November 1947, the United Nations voted to divide Palestine into two states. One of the states would be Jewish, and the other state Arab. While most Arabs objected to this agreement, Israelis welcomed it. **Israel** declared itself an independent country on May 14, 1948.

Show What You Know

Think about the history of the Jews. After so many years without a homeland, what do you think was the main event that led to the creation of the state of Israel? Was it the Zionist movement, the spread of anti-Semitism, the Holocaust, or another reason? Be sure to consider what was happening in the European countries economically and politically at the time. Use historical facts and write your response below.

_____

_____

_____

_____

_____

_____

_____

_____

_____

_____

_____

_____

_____

_____

_____

_____

_____

_____

_____

_____

_____

_____

Lesson Practice

Thinking It Through

1. Before the state of Israel was declared in 1948, Palestine was ruled by the

   A. anti-Semites.

   B. British Empire.

   C. Arab armies.

   D. Zionist movement.

   One of the reasons that Palestine was available for the new Jewish homeland of Israel is that in 1948 it was not controlled by any of the groups that were fighting over it. An outside power had control.

2. In 1881, violent anti-Jewish riots began spreading from Russia to parts of Eastern and Central Europe. By which name are these riots known?

   A. Ottomans

   B. racism

   C. hostilities

   D. pogroms

   HINT *The Ottomans were people that lived during the Ottoman Empire. Racism was the belief that led to the riots.*

3. All of the following are examples of anti-Semitism EXCEPT

   A. the Balfour Declaration.

   B. the Dreyfus Affair.

   C. the Holocaust.

   D. restrictions on Jewish immigration.

4. Who was the leader of the Zionist movement?

   A. Adolf Hitler

   B. Theodor Herzl

   C. the mayor of Vienna

   D. Alfred Dreyfus

18 Israeli and Arab Conflict

 SS7H2.c

May 15, 1948, is known to Arabs as "al-Nakba," or the Catastrophe. That is the day when the state of Israel was declared and the last of the British troops left the region. The very next day, five Arab armies from surrounding countries invaded the new state. These forces were then defeated by the Israeli army. Over the next several years, the Arab countries surrounding Israel and Palestine competed to lead Arab forces against the new Israel.

The Conflict Continues

In 1964, the **Palestine Liberation Organization (PLO)** was formed. The PLO was made up of several Palestinian political groups from different countries. Their goal was to take Palestine back from the Israelis. In 1969, Yasser Arafat became the leader of the PLO. Five years earlier, Fatah, a secret armed group that Arafat had founded, made its first attacks on Israel. Arafat served as the leader of the PLO until his death in 2004. During the 35 years of Arafat's leadership, Israel elected several different leaders, known as prime ministers.

In 1967, the Six-Day War occurred in June and changed the face of the Southwest Asian conflict. Israel was able to double the amount of land it controlled. This also helped to spread hope and confidence throughout all of Israel and to its supporters.

Another 500,000 Palestinians fled their homes during this conflict, joining the hundreds of thousands already displaced by years of fighting between Jewish and Arab forces. Many of these people ended up in Egypt, Syria, Lebanon, and Jordan.

For the next several years, and still today, Israeli and Arab forces have attacked and counterattacked one another. Attempts at peace agreements have been made with the help of other nations, including the United States. So far, no treaty or agreement has been successful in bringing peace to the region.

In 1971, the PLO was expelled from its base in Jordan by the Jordanian army. They moved to Lebanon. A terrorist group called "Black September" was formed by Palestinian militants. The following year, at the Olympics in Munich, Germany, this group took 11 Israeli athletes hostage. All of the athletes were killed, along with five of the terrorists and one policeman.

Attempts at Peace

Menachem Begin became prime minister of Israel in 1977, during the U.S. presidency of Jimmy Carter. President Carter helped Prime Minister Begin and Egyptian President Anwar Sadat work out an agreement. The agreement is called the Camp David Accords.

The three leaders met at Camp David in the United States. Begin agreed to remove all Israeli troops from the Sinai Peninsula and return the land to Egypt. Other Arab countries were not happy about this agreement. They stopped doing business with Egypt. In 1981, Sadat was assassinated by troops in the Egyptian army.

In 1982, the Israeli army invaded Lebanon. Led by defense minister Ariel Sharon, they drove the PLO out of Lebanon. Many of the Palestinians who had settled in Lebanon were living there in refugee camps. When the PLO left, these camps had no military troops to defend them.

During this time, a Palestinian refugee camp in Lebanon was attacked by Lebanese allies of the Israelis. Hundreds of refugees were killed. The Israeli government decided that Sharon should have acted to prevent the massacre. Because of this event, Sharon gave up his job as defense minister.

Hezbollah and **Hamas** are two Arab groups that were founded in the mid-1980s. Hezbollah is from Lebanon. Hamas is based in the West Bank and the Gaza Strip. Both groups are supported by Syria and Iran and are made up of Muslims. Over the last 25 years, both groups have each led attacks on Israel. These attacks have often been very violent and have killed many civilians.

The late 1980s and the 1990s saw continued fighting between Israelis and Arabs. Often civilians were involved, and thousands have been killed. There have been treaties and agreements, but unfortunately, they have not led to peace in the region.

In 2004, Arafat died and was succeeded by Mahmoud Abbas. In 2005, President Abbas successfully convinced Hamas and other groups to temporarily and unofficially stop their attacks on Israelis. President Abbas and Israeli Prime Minister Ariel Sharon agreed to a ceasefire, which is when fighting stops between two groups. Sharon agreed to withdraw Israeli forces and settlers from a contested region of land called the Gaza Strip. By early September of 2005, the Israelis had left, and Palestinians took control of the region.

In July of 2006, war broke out again between Hezbollah and Israeli forces. Hezbollah kidnapped two Israeli soldiers and killed eight, and Israel responded with a full-scale attack on Hezbollah's bases in Lebanon. The fighting lasted about a month. Hezbollah proved to have a larger and better-organized army than the Israelis had believed.

Israelis and Palestinians have fought over the Gaza Strip.

The United Nations helped both sides agree to end the fighting, but not for long. Palestinian militants in the Gaza Strip continued firing rockets into Israel. Israel responded by invading the Gaza Strip in 2008. Israeli forces have since withdrawn from the Gaza Strip, but the larger conflict over control of the land continues.

Show What You Know

The Israeli-Arab conflict is in the news almost daily. Have you ever heard of this conflict before reading this lesson? Write out what you have heard before and what you thought of this news. If you have not heard of the Israeli-Arab conflict in the news before, write down ways that you could try to learn more about it in the future. Finally, write down how you understand the conflict differently after studying it in this lesson. Have your ideas about it changed?

_____

_____

_____

_____

_____

_____

_____

_____

_____

_____

_____

_____

_____

_____

_____

_____

Lesson Practice

DIRECTIONS
Circle the letter of the best answer for each item.

Thinking It Through

1. The Palestine Liberation Organization (PLO) was formed in 1964 to take Palestine back from

   A. the British Empire.

   B. Egypt.

   C. Israel.

   D. Syria.

   Large portions of Palestine were given to the Jewish people in 1948 by the UN. After that, the Israelis fought many wars to defend the land from Arabs and Muslims in the region.

2. The Six-Day War of 1967 between the PLO and Israel was a conflict over control of land. Which country gained territory as a result?

   A. Palestine

   B. Israel

   C. Lebanon

   D. Jordan

   HINT *After the Six-Day War, several Arab nations in the region sought peace treaties with Israel.*

3. All of the following are Arab groups EXCEPT

   A. the PLO.

   B. Hamas.

   C. Hezbollah.

   D. the Israeli army.

4. Who was the U.S. president during the Camp David Accords?

   A. Bill Clinton

   B. Jimmy Carter

   C. George Bush

   D. Arthur Balfour

Lesson

19 The Impact of Oil and the Southwest Asian Wars

 SS7G7.a, SS7H2.d

Countries use oil to produce gasoline, jet fuel, and heat for homes and businesses. Countries in North Africa and the Persian Gulf export more oil than most other countries in the world. The control of oil reserves has been an issue in many of the wars fought in Southwest Asia during the 20th century. Many countries have been involved in wars in Southwest Asia.

Persian Gulf War

The Persian Gulf War was a war between Iraq and a group of about thirty other nations. Iraq accused Kuwait of stealing Iraqi oil by drilling under the border between the two countries. Iraq invaded Kuwait in August of 1990, under the direction of Iraqi President Saddam Hussein. The Iraqi army took control of Kuwait in a very short amount of time.

The United Nations responded to the Iraqi invasion by demanding that Iraq withdraw its troops from Kuwait. The United Nations used the Iraqi economy to try to convince the country to withdraw. They did this by cutting off trade to the country. Iraq did not withdraw. Many citizens of Kuwait fled the country during the Iraqi occupation.

The United States and other countries began sending troops to Saudi Arabia over the next few months. The United Nations set a date for Iraq to leave Kuwait. Iraq rejected this date and refused to back down. The Iraqis remained in Kuwait after the date. The U.S. and other nations attacked the Iraqi forces in January of 1991. The Iraqi army was defeated in less than two months. Iraq was then directed to recognize Kuwait's sovereignty and destroy all weapons of mass destruction.

U.S. Invasion of Afghanistan

On September 11, 2001, al-Qaeda attacked two targets in the United States. **Al-Qaeda** is a group of radical Islamic terrorists based largely in Afghanistan. They hijacked four airplanes and crashed two of them into the World Trade Center in New York. The third airplane crashed into the Pentagon in Virginia, and the fourth crashed in rural Pennsylvania, before reaching its intended target of the White House. These terrorist attacks killed nearly 3,000 people.

Investigations into the attack have named Osama bin Laden as its organizer. U.S. President George W. Bush called on other countries to help wage a war on terrorism. The first goal of those nations that joined the U.S. was to find bin Laden, whom they believed to be in Afghanistan, even though most of the people carrying out the attacks were from Saudi Arabia.

Duplicating any part of this book is prohibited by law.

In October 2001, U.S. and British troops invaded Afghanistan in search of bin Laden. They bombed places where bin Laden was known to be. Over the years, millions of people from Afghanistan have been left homeless because of the many wars that have taken place in their country. After the invasion, more than three million refugees returned to their homes. The U.S.-led forces still struggle to control portions of the country. The goal is to help Afghan people to reestablish stability in their country so U.S. forces can leave. At the time of publication, Osama bin Laden has not been found.

Iraq War

Saddam Hussein was still the president of Iraq at the time of the invasion of Afghanistan. Officials in the U.S. government feared connections between the Hussein regime and al-Qaeda. They were also afraid that Iraq was building **weapons of mass destruction (WMDs)**, such as chemical or biological weapons. The United Nations sent inspectors to Iraq to check for WMDs. Hussein was given a chance to prove he was not developing WMDs. He ignored this opportunity. In 2002, the United States Congress passed an Iraq War Resolution that authorized the president to go forward with a war in Iraq.

In March 2003, the U.S. bombed targets in the Iraqi capital of Baghdad. The next day, British, Australian, and Polish soldiers joined the U.S. in invading Iraq and defeating the Iraqi military. This effort was known as Operation Iraqi Freedom. Saddam Hussein was captured, and his rule ended. He was sentenced to death in 2006, after being tried for killing 148 people in the Iraqi village of Dujail. Iraq under Hussein was previously involved in a long war against Iran in which chemical weapons were used against the Kurds and Iranians. He was also responsible for the deaths of hundreds of thousands of Iraqis. Hussein's death sentence was carried out later in 2006.

Weapons of mass destruction have not been found in Iraq. It is difficult to determine how many Iraqis have died since the invasion, but more than a half million Iraqis may have died according to one study. Many deaths are due to different groups fighting each other to gain power or the disruption of adequate medical care. As of the end of 2009, over 4,000 American soldiers had been killed and over 20,000 had been wounded in Iraq.

The United States plans to withdraw its soldiers from Iraq by 2011.

Show What You Know

Put all the facts you learned in this lesson into a timeline. Once you have the events summarized in your timeline, think about cause and effect. What causes and effects can you identify in the timeline?

_____

_____

_____

_____

_____

_____

_____

_____

Lesson Practice

Thinking It Through

1. Countries in which region(s) export the MOST oil worldwide?

   A. Pacific Northwest

   B. Antarctica and North Pole

   C. North Africa and Persian Gulf

   D. Southern and Eastern Asia

   This region contains large natural oil reserves. Many leaders in this region belong to OPEC, an organization that coordinates petroleum production. Many wars are fought in this region, some of which are due to oil issues.

2. What was one reason the Bush administration had for going to war in Iraq in 2003?

   A. They suspected the Iraqi government of having ties to terrorism.

   B. They wanted to stop Iraq from invading Saudi Arabia.

   C. They were responding to Iraqi attacks on the World Trade Center.

   D. They thought that Osama bin Laden was hiding in Iraq.

   HINT *Terrorism was responsible for the attacks on September 11, 2001.*

3. What was the result of the Persian Gulf War?

   A. The United Nations permitted trade with Iraq.

   B. The United States found weapons of mass destruction.

   C. The Kuwaiti army was defeated.

   D. The Iraqi army was defeated.

4. Which of the following BEST describes Operation Iraqi Freedom?

   A. a struggle between two neighboring countries over oil rights

   B. a search for weapons of mass destruction

   C. a global struggle against today's slave trade

   D. a search for Osama bin Laden

20 Physical Features of Southwest Asia

SS7G5.a–b, SS7G7.b

Southwest Asia, otherwise known as the Middle East, is a large region with many deserts and plains. Today, about 300 million people live in the region, and most live in urban centers. Deserts include the Arabian Desert, the Libyan Desert, and the Syrian Desert. There are also many mountain ranges in Southwest Asia. These include major mountains in Turkey, Iran, and Iraq. There are several inland seas, as well. These include the Caspian Sea on the northern side of Iran, and the Black Sea, north of Turkey.

Southwest Asia is a large region with many different climates. The northern coast of Iran gets a lot of rainfall. Some desert areas get no rain at all. Since so much of the region is relatively dry, the location of rivers has had a great impact on where people live and the kind of work they do.

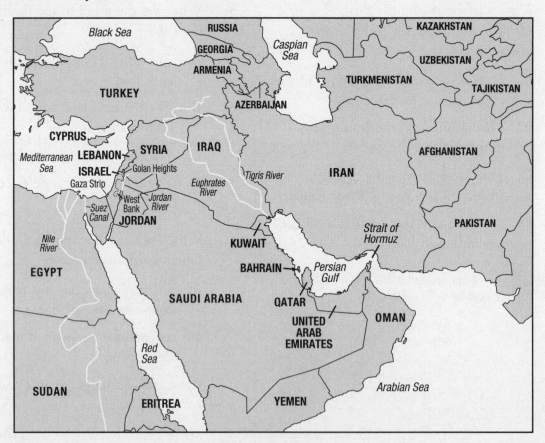

Israel

Israel contains several different geographical areas. There are mountains in the north. This region of mountains is called Galilee. A region of farmlands is south of Galilee. There is also desert in southern Israel. There are plains along the coast. Most of the cities are on the coast of the Mediterranean Sea, where the major ports and industries are located.

The Jordan River is the border between Jordan and the West Bank. It empties into the Dead Sea. The Dead Sea is the lowest point on Earth's surface. The Gulf of Aqaba is at the southern tip of Israel. The gulf opens into the Red Sea. The port of Elat is on the Gulf of Aqaba. This location makes the port of Elat important to Israeli trade. It is the only place where Israeli merchants can reach the Red Sea for shipping purposes.

Saudi Arabia

Saudi Arabia lies to the south of Jordan. Saudi Arabia is the largest Southwest Asian country. More than half of the country is desert. The desert is in the southern, eastern, and northern parts of Saudi Arabia. Saudi Arabia also has coastal plains in the east along the Persian Gulf. These plains are good for farming. In the western highlands, there are mountains, but there is some farming in this region, too. Saudi Arabia has no lakes or rivers that are permanent. Rainfall creates temporary rivers and streams, however. Most of Saudi Arabia has a hot desert climate.

Much of Saudi Arabia is desert.

The eastern plains of Saudi Arabia are the location of large deposits of oil. They provide the country's primary income source. Much of the Saudi Arabian population lives near the country's oil industry and the ports on the Persian Gulf. Many people lived in this region even before oil was discovered there. Natural springs are found in the east. Such springs allowed people to settle and farm in this region. Many other parts of the country are not fit to live in because of the hot climate.

Iran

Iran is located across the Persian Gulf from Saudi Arabia. It is the second biggest Middle Eastern country. It shares a border with Iraq, Kuwait, and Turkey in the west. In the east, it borders Pakistan and Afghanistan. On the northern side of Iran are the Caspian Sea, Armenia, Azerbaijan, and Turkmenistan. To the south is the Persian Gulf, which flows through the Strait of Hormuz and out into the Arabian Sea. Much of Iran is mountains and plains. The mountains are mostly around the country's edges. The middle of the country is mostly plains and desert.

Some mountain areas have farming during rainy periods. The coastal plains lie between the mountains and the Caspian Sea. The mountains in Iran are part of an earthquake zone. Like Saudi Arabia, Iran has large oil deposits near the Persian Gulf. This wealth makes the Gulf a good place for industry and transport. Iran's rivers are useful for irrigating crops, but not for shipping or travel.

Iraq

Iraq is north of Saudi Arabia and west of Iran. In the southeast, Iraq has access to the Persian Gulf. Iraq has mountains, swamps, deserts, and large rivers. The Tigris and the Euphrates Rivers flow on either side of the region in Iraq, once known as Mesopotamia. Both rivers flow across the entire country. In the southeast, the rivers are useful for travel and irrigation. Both rivers flow into Iraq from Syria and Turkey. Much of their strength is used up for farming in those countries before the rivers reach Iraq.

Two boys sit by the Euphrates River.

Northeastern Iraq has mountains. The south and west are mainly desert. Many major cities are located near the fertile areas around the two rivers. Iraq also has oil deposits in the southeast that provide the country's main source of income.

Jordan

Jordan is to the east of Israel. Most of Jordan is desert. Jordan has mountains in the south along the border with Saudi Arabia. In the west is the Jordan Valley. This is a rich farming area. Jordan also has some farming in the northern highlands. The Jordan River and several others provide a good source of irrigation for farming. The capital and other major cities are in this region. The climate of Jordan is hot and dry in summer and cool in winter. Like Israel, Jordan has access to the Gulf of Aqaba in the south. The gulf is also an important feature for Jordanian trade.

Kuwait

Kuwait is on the coast of the Persian Gulf. The country is surrounded by Iraq and Saudi Arabia. Kuwait is a very small country. It is only one hundred and twenty miles across at its widest point. Much of Kuwait is desert, but also includes islands off the shore in the gulf. Kuwait Bay is a deep water bay in the Persian Gulf. The depth of the bay contributes to Kuwait's prominence as a center of shipping and sailing in the Gulf area. Like other countries bordering the Gulf, Kuwait has large oil deposits that are the main source of the country's income. There is little farming in Kuwait. There are no sources of fresh water. Oil revenues support Kuwait's economy.

Syria

Syria lies on the Mediterranean Sea, south of Turkey and west of Iraq. Like Iraq, Syria benefits from the Euphrates River. The Euphrates flows through the northeastern part of Syria. The country also uses the Euphrates to generate electrical power. Syria has rich gas and mineral deposits that provide much of the country's income. However, pollution from these industries has made it difficult for the country to get fresh water for people to drink. Syria has often fought with other countries for control of water sources like the Euphrates River.

Lebanon

Lebanon's entire west coast is on the Mediterranean Sea. It is southwest of Syria and north of Israel. The country's coastal plains and mountains provide excellent sources of fresh water. Melted snow from the mountains provides an abundance of water for farming. The country has a few mineral deposits, but not enough to support industry. Much of the economy is based on agriculture.

Afghanistan

Afghanistan is east of Iran and north of Pakistan. Mountains cover most of the country. The climate of Afghanistan is harsh. Summer temperatures are very hot and winters are extremely cold. The climate and the landscape make farming very difficult. Much of the economy in Afghanistan is based on the country's deposits of minerals and precious stones.

Show What You Know

Without looking back at the lesson, try to fill in this map with labels for the names of countries and bodies of water. When you have filled in all you can from memory, check your answers, make corrections, and fill in the rest of the map.

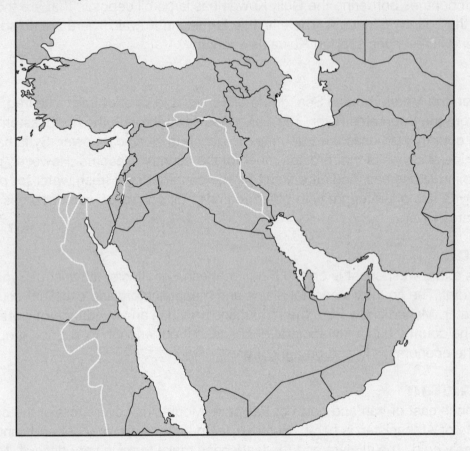

Lesson Practice

DIRECTIONS
Circle the letter of the best answer for each item.

Thinking It Through

1. Why is the port of Elat important to Israeli trade?

   In order for a country to trade goods, it must have access to waterways that lead to other countries.

   A. It is only accessible for a few days during the year.

   B. It is the only place Israeli merchants can reach the Red Sea for shipping purposes.

   C. It is the only place Israeli fishermen can catch fish.

   D. It is the only connection to the Mediterranean Sea.

---

2. Which of these statements describes the importance of Saudi Arabia's location on the Persian Gulf?

   A. It has made Saudi Arabia's economy heavily dependent upon imports.

   B. It has allowed the Saudi Arabian people to migrate easily.

   C. It has given Saudi Arabia access to ports on the Gulf.

   D. It has helped Saudi Arabia build a powerful navy.

   HINT *The oil produced in Saudi Arabia is a crucial export for the economy.*

3. How does Southwest Asia today compare to the past?

   A. Its population has mostly shifted to living in urban areas.

   B. Farming is the basis of most of the Southwest Asian economy.

   C. Its climate is mostly cold, and there is a lot of snow.

   D. It is a land of plentiful fresh water that is never polluted.

4. Which of these geographic features is located in Iraq?

   A. the Tigris River

   B. the Port of Aqaba

   C. the Strait of Hormuz

   D. the Suez Canal

21 Southwest Asian Environmental Policies

 SS7G6.a

There are many serious environmental problems today in Southwest Asia. Governments play a role in both causing and trying to solve these problems.

Major Environmental Issues

The water supply in Southwest Asia is very limited. Finding a source of fresh water for farming and drinking is a struggle throughout the region. For example, Israel has very few fresh water sources. The Sea of Galilee provides its primary supply of drinking water. Many Southwest Asian countries must use desalination to get fresh water. **Desalination** is a process for removing the salt from salt water in order to make it suitable for drinking and farming.

There are very few major rivers in the region. The Tigris, Euphrates, and Nile rivers are the longest and most powerful. These rivers run through just a few countries of the entire region. Rivers are the main source of water for drinking and for electrical power in many Southwest Asian countries. Countries without major rivers must also find other ways to generate electricity.

Pollution is also a problem. Many Southwest Asian cities are based around ports. These cities usually have major industries and many factories. Ports make it easier to ship the things produced by industries. Port cities with major industries usually pollute their water supplies. For example, oil is the main export in Southwest Asia. Huge ships and oil spills pollute the waters of the Persian Gulf.

Many natural resources are in the ground and must be taken out. The process of removing them is called **extraction**. Oil is the largest natural resource in Southwest Asia. Drilling oil from the ground requires heavy machinery that often endangers the environment. The process of refining oil also creates pollution. **Refining** oil means making oil from the ground ready to make fuel to operate machines. Refining oil produces toxic chemicals. This is an enormous problem for the environment in Southwest Asia.

Water Supply

Southwest Asian countries often get into disputes over their policies on water rights and other natural resources. **Water rights** are agreements about how countries can use the water in a region. Water rights often cause political disputes.

Israel, Jordan, and the Palestinians on the West Bank, all depend on many of the same scarce water resources. Israel has the most military power, so it has been most effective in claiming water. Much Israeli water is also cleaned after it is used once, and is then reused. Ways have to be found to make sure that everyone has access to enough water.

The Euphrates River flows through Turkey, Syria, and Iraq. These countries all rely on the Euphrates for farming and for electricity. The river begins in Turkey and flows to the Persian Gulf. Turkey built two dams on the Euphrates in 1984 to harness its power for electricity. These dams make the river less powerful. Syria also built a dam on the Euphrates. By the time the river reaches Iraq, it is much smaller and less powerful than it was originally. The water supply in Iraq is diminished, and farming is very difficult. In 1975, a war almost broke out between Syria and Iraq over water rights.

Oil Industries

Disputes over access to other natural resources, like oil, also cause conflict. The largest source of oil in the world is the region bordering the Persian Gulf. All the countries that border the Persian Gulf have large oil industries. Many wars have been fought over oil in Southwest Asia. These wars have had a major impact on the environment. For example, much of the oil refining machinery in Iraq was badly damaged in the Persian Gulf War, in 1991. The Iraqi government did not repair the equipment that makes refining oil safer for the environment. For years, pollution from Iraqi oil refineries leaked into the water supply and into the air. Today, the Iraqi oil industry is not productive because of the current war in Iraq. However, many of Iraq's oil refineries were destroyed and burned during the war. As a result, the air was polluted.

Oil extraction can cause pollution.

During the first Gulf War, Iraq used pollution as a strategy for fighting. Iraqi soldiers dumped over three hundred gallons of oil into the Persian Gulf. They also burned hundreds of oil wells in order to keep the U.S. from taking control of their oil industry.

Oil is the basis of most of the economy of Southwest Asia, but pollution from the oil industry is one of the biggest threats to its environment. This pollution endangers the water supply in particular. Since there is not much fresh water in the region, these environmental problems directly affect the lives of people in Southwest Asia.

Show What You Know

Make two lists. The first list should include reasons why oil is important to Southwest Asia. The second should list reasons why fresh water is important. Which do you think is more important to Southwest Asia—oil or water? Why?

_____

_____

_____

_____

_____

_____

_____

_____

_____

_____

_____

_____

_____

_____

_____

_____

_____

_____

_____

_____

_____

_____

Lesson Practice

DIRECTIONS
Circle the letter of the best answer for each item.

Thinking It Through

1. Which statement BEST explains why the Tigris and Euphrates rivers have been a source of conflict for many years?

   A. They both form borders between Iraq and Iran.

   B. They are the quickest routes to the Mediterranean Sea in Southwest Asia.

   C. They make up most of the water supply for Turkey, Syria, and Iraq.

   D. They are frequented by pirates.

   Neither river reaches Iran. The Euphrates begins in Turkey and flows southeast.

2. Which statement BEST defines the term "water rights"?

   A. laws that say who can use the water in a region

   B. laws that tell which side of a river ships can sail on

   C. laws that protect the natural environment from abuses

   D. laws concerning the bottling and distribution of bottled water

   HINT *Water rights are disputed in regions where the water supply is short.*

3. Which is one way Israel has used natural resources for political purposes?

   A. burning hundreds of oil wells

   B. controlling the water supply

   C. directing the flow of volcanic lava

   D. starting forest fires

4. Which statement BEST describes many of the Persian Gulf countries today?

   A. They are overcrowded.

   B. They lack adequate housing.

   C. They have major oil deposits.

   D. They are agricultural centers.

22 Cultural Features of Southwest Asia

 SS7G8.a–e

There are a wide variety of ethnic and religious groups in Southwest Asia. An ethnic group is a cultural community of people with common ancestry, often sharing common religion, language, and traditions. A religious group is a community of people sharing the same religion.

Arab peoples make up almost the entire population of Jordan, Syria, Egypt, Lebanon, and other countries of Southwest Asia. Arab culture has a long history and rich traditions. Many other cultures also live in the region. Christianity and Judaism are major religions practiced in Southwest Asia. However, most people there are Muslims. This means that they practice the religion of Islam. Ninety percent of people in the region are Muslims.

Arab

Arabs comprise most of the population of Southwest Asia. However, many Arabs also live in North Africa, Canada, Europe, and the United States. Most Arabs practice Islam and speak Arabic. Small numbers of Arabs practice other religions. Islam consists mostly of two different groups. The majority of Muslims practice Sunni Islam. Others practice Shi'as Islam. Sunnis and Shi'as disagree about who is in charge of the Muslim world. Sunnis believe that new leaders should be chosen but do not have to come from Muhammad's family. The Shi'a believe that new leaders need to be descendents of Muhammad.

Jewish

Israel is home for much of the Jewish population in Southwest Asia. Many of the people who live in Israel today were born there. However, the ancestors of these people moved to Israel from many other countries, often from other Southwest Asian countries. Much of this migration happened during the 20th century, after the formation of Israel in the late 1940s. Jewish people differ in their religious beliefs, though most practice some form of Judaism. For example, some Jews believe that Jewish people who convert to another religion should not be considered Jewish anymore. The **Law of Return** in Israel says that a Jew from any other country can automatically have citizenship in Israel. However, sometimes Jews who no longer practice Judaism have been denied the Law of Return.

Berber

The **Berbers** are another minority group in the region. Most Berbers live in North Africa and were the first group to settle that region. They still live a traditional way of life today. Berbers have their own languages. Many Berber tribes live in the mountains and deserts. Most Berbers living in mountainous areas are farmers. Berbers who live in the desert tend to live near an oasis. Berbers who do not farm are nomadic. The majority of Berber tribes are Muslim. Some Berbers practice other religions, too.

Berber woman and child

Druze

The **Druze** are an ethnic group that is based on religion. The religion of the Druze is based on Islam and other religions. The Druze live mostly in Lebanon. Some Druze also live in Israel, Jordan, and Syria. The Druze keep their religious practices secret. The people are split into two social groups. The first group is comprised of people who are not allowed to see the holy books of the Druze. This group makes up most of the Druze population. The second group is composed of spiritual leaders. Many of these leaders are women. The Druze believe that men are spiritually inferior to women.

Bedouin

The **Bedouin** are another ethnic group. They speak Arabic. Many Bedouin used to be nomadic. Now, the Bedouin live mostly in Saudi Arabia, Syria, Jordan, and Iraq. They live mostly in cities and are not nomadic. Bedouin tribes are ruled by tribal leaders called sheikhs. Most Bedouins practice Islam. The Bedouin are well known for their dress and music, which is mostly sung. Music is used to perform traditional Bedouin ceremonies.

Two Bedouin men

Kurdish

Southwest Asia is also home to the Kurdish people. The **Kurds** live in several countries throughout the region. These include Turkey, Syria, Iraq, and Iran. Almost one-fifth of the population of Turkey is Kurdish. The Kurdish religion used to be made up of a mixture of several different religions. Most Kurds today are Muslims. Kurdish Muslims are usually less strict about certain Islamic practices. For example, there are fewer laws for how Kurdish women should dress than there are for Iranian and Arab women. Kurds share many aspects of their culture with Iranians.

Turkish

The **Turks** are an ethnic group based on language—Turkish. They live mostly in Turkey and Iran. Most of the people who live in Turkey are of Turkish descent. Most Turks practice some form of Islam. Like Kurds, Turkish people are rarely strict about their Islamic practices. However, Kurds and Turks in Turkey often fight over issues not related to religion.

A mosque in Istanbul, Turkey

The Turkish people are well known for their architecture. Mosques in Turkey are a good example of Turkish architecture.

Persian

The **Persians** are an ethnic group that lived in Iran before the arrival of Islam in the 7th century. Persians make up about half of Iran's current population. They have their own language called Persian, or Farsi. Most Persians in Iran today practice Shi'a Islam, but some are Sunni and other religions. Persian women have faced many challenges as a result of strict cultural and religious practices. Through struggle, Persian women have increased their personal freedoms over the past forty years. Persian art and architecture is also well known. Many people consider Persian rugs to be among the finest in the world.

A Persian rug

Armenian

Armenians are an ethnic group that lives mostly in Armenia and the surrounding areas. In addition, many Armenians live outside of Southwest Asia. Armenians speak a different kind of Armenian depending on where they live. Most Southwest Asian Armenians identify themselves as Christians. This means that Armenians differ a lot from other ethnic groups in the region. Armenian culture has been greatly influenced by the surrounding cultures, like Russian and Turkish. They are known for their literature, dance, and lace making.

Literacy and Development

Education is free in many countries in Southwest Asia. Many students are required to attend school through high school. However, fighting often keeps students from showing up at school. Many students also live so far from the schools that getting to school is difficult. The literacy rates for people over fifteen years of age are 77% in Syria, 79% in Iran, 95% in Israel, and 79% in Saudi Arabia.

The literacy rates in Israel are higher than in other Southwest Asian countries. In all of these countries, more men tend to be able to read and write than women. This is especially true in Syria, Iran, and Saudi Arabia. Overall in some countries women's education is not valued as much as men's education. Furthermore, women receive a different education than men in some areas.

Literacy has a large impact on a country's standard of living. For example, an increase in the literacy rate often leads to an increase in individual rights. Literacy rates also have an impact on a country's economy. Countries with higher literacy rates usually have more developed economies and a wider variety of good-paying jobs. This leads to a higher standard of living for the population.

Southwest Asian Art and Music

Bedouin culture and Islam have had a large impact on the arts in Saudi Arabia. The sacred text of Islam, the *Qur'an*, is probably the most influential work of Arabic literature. Many Muslims consider pictures of people or animals to be sinful. For that reason, art and architecture in the Arab world feature geometric shapes and Arabic writing. Singers from Saudi Arabia are very popular in Southwest Asia.

The theme of much Israeli art is Israel's struggle for independence. Music is very popular in Israel. Israeli musicians and orchestras are well-known around the world.

Two boys read the Qur'an

Show What You Know

Make a list of the different ethnic groups in Southwest Asia. Try to label, from memory, which groups practice Islam, Christianity, or Judaism. Then list any other cultural characteristics you can remember about each group. Check your answers against the lesson, and fill in anything you did not know from memory.

_____

_____

_____

_____

_____

_____

_____

_____

_____

_____

_____

_____

_____

_____

_____

_____

_____

_____

_____

Lesson Practice

Circle the letter of the best answer for each item.

Thinking It Through

1. Most Southwest Asian Jews live in which nation?

Iran, Syria, and Lebanon are Muslim nations. Israel was created so that Jews could live there.

   A. Israel

   B. Iran

   C. Syria

   D. Lebanon

---

2. Which statement about Southwest Asia today is true?

   A. Only a few different ethnic groups live there.

   B. The majority of its residents are Arabs.

   C. It has very good literacy rates.

   D. Much of its economy is based on tourism.

HINT *Tourism is not a booming business in Southwest Asia.*

3. Literacy rates in Southwest Asia have risen dramatically in the 20th century. What will MOST LIKELY happen as a result of the rising literacy rates?

   A. The economy will improve.

   B. The unemployment rate will also rise.

   C. The birth rate will soar.

   D. Ethnic groups will stop fighting.

4. Which statement explains why the art and architecture of Saudi Arabia feature geometric shapes and writing?

   A. Geometric shapes can more easily withstand the desert heat.

   B. Saudi Arabians prefer math to drawing and painting.

   C. Arab art is some of the most experimental art in the world.

   D. Muslims believe that an image of a person or animal is sinful.

23 Southwest Asian Governments

 SS7CG5.a

Religion plays an important role in Southwest Asian governments. Countries such as Iran and Saudi Arabia have based their systems of government on religion. Religion is important even in countries that do not base their governments on religion. Many political parties in Southwest Asia are religious in nature. Many parties represent different branches of Islam. Since the majority of the people in the region are Muslim, religion also influences the way people vote in popular elections.

While religion is important throughout the region, the specific form of government differs from country to country. In terms of voting rights and personal freedoms, the role of citizens varies widely as well.

Israel

Israel has a parliamentary democracy. The head of state is the president, who actually does not have much power. The Israeli prime minister is the head of government.

The legislature elects the president. The president then chooses the head of the largest political party to be the prime minister. The prime minister must organize a coalition to govern. A coalition is a group of several different political parties that have to cooperate in order to make decisions. This type of government is known as a **coalition government**.

The Israeli legislature is called the **Knesset**. The Knesset holds most of the power in Israeli government. The Knesset consists of 120 members. Israelis, 18 years of age and older, elect these officials by popular vote.

Israeli law protects the rights and freedoms of its citizens. In this way, Israel is similar to the United States, Canada, and European democracies. Israel's Declaration of Independence states that all citizens should have equal rights, regardless of sex, race, or religion. While this is not a legally binding document, much of Israeli law has been based on its principles. Israel's Supreme Court has issued many rulings protecting basic freedoms such as freedom of speech and freedom of assembly.

Saudi Arabia

In contrast to Israel's parliamentary democracy, Saudi Arabia is a monarchy governed by Islamic Shari'ah Law. The country has no formal constitution. The Basic Law of 1992 declared that Saudi Arabia should be ruled by a king, with laws based on the *Qur'an*. No political parties are allowed, and there are no national elections to choose leaders.

In 2004, however, the Saudi government allowed a small change when it began allowing men who are 21 and older to vote for half of their local officials. Men can also vote for one-third of the members of the legislature.

Saudi Arabia remains far from a democratic state, however. Saudi kings are both heads of state and heads of government. Voters have no say in choosing this leader. The king has a cabinet called the Council of Ministers. The Council mostly consists of members of the royal family.

The Saudi legislature is called the Consultative Council. There are 120 members of the Council. There is also a Council chairman. The king chooses two-thirds of the members of the Council. Council members serve terms of four years.

While Saudi men play a small role in participating in the government, Saudi women have few rights in Saudi society. Women cannot vote, and most are not allowed to drive cars or participate in sports.

Most Saudi women wear chadors because of Shari'ah Law. Women are not allowed to vote or participate in government.

Iran

The Islamic Republic of Iran is a theocratic republic. A **theocracy** is a government run by religious leaders, while a republic is run by elected representatives. As Iran's name implies, the country's government is a mix of theocracy and republic.

In 1979, the Islamic, or Iranian, revolution overthrew the monarchy that had ruled Iran for centuries. Leaders of the revolution wrote a new constitution for Iran, putting in place its current system of government. The head of Iran's government state is the Supreme Leader, who is always an **ayatollah**, or recognized religious authority.

The Supreme Leader is chosen by the Assembly of Experts and holds the position for life. The Assembly consists of 86 religious scholars. The people elect the Assembly and the president by popular vote. The president governs based on the religious guidance of the ayatollah. The president can serve two terms of four years each. Iran's legislature is called the Consultative Assembly. Citizens fifteen and older can vote for the 290 members of the Assembly.

While Iranian citizens have important rights, the government sometimes uses force to suppress those rights. When President Mahmoud Ahmadinejad ran for re-election in 2009, for example, many citizens were convinced his party committed fraud, claiming to have gotten more votes than it really did. Hundreds of thousands of people took to the streets to protest the unfair elections. Iranian police violently attacked the protestors. The government also censored newspapers and Web sites in an effort to silence opposition.

Show What You Know

Fill in the chart below.

Country	Type of Government	Who Can Vote
Israel		
Saudi Arabia		
Iran		

Lesson Practice

Thinking It Through

1. In 1979, the Islamic revolution overthrew the monarchy of which country?

   A. Jordan

   B. Turkey

   C. Iran

   D. Saudi Arabia

The revolution transformed this country into a theocratic republic. The ayatollah is an important figure. Saudi Arabia's king is Abdallah bin Abd al-Aziz. The Turkish Republic began in 1923.

2. A religious leader oversees the state of Iran. By which title is this leader known?

   A. president

   B. shah

   C. king

   D. ayatollah

   HINT *Remember that Iran does not have a monarch.*

3. Which statement about Saudi Arabia today is true?

   A. Its government is based primarily on religion.

   B. It is ruled by a religious leader and a symbolic president.

   C. Its citizens can vote for all government officials.

   D. Its citizens can now vote for some government officials.

4. Which of the following BEST describes the government of Israel?

   A. It is ruled by a coalition of several different political parties.

   B. It has only one political party, and the president has the most power.

   C. Its legislature serves a mostly symbolic role.

   D. It is ruled by monarchs who select the members of the legislature.

24 Southwest Asian Trade

 SS7E6.a–d

Before the 1950s, Southwest Asia had a very strong agricultural industry. Today, most countries in the region depend heavily on voluntary trade. Southwest Asia must import much of its food and other products for daily life. Over half of the food eaten in Southwest Asia is produced outside the region. The region does not have many highly developed industries besides oil. Without trade with other nations, countries in Southwest Asia would suffer.

Some Southwest Asian countries are trying to trade more with other nations in order to improve their economies. For example, twelve countries including Israel, the Palestinian National Authority, and Syria signed a trade agreement with the European Union in 1995. The purpose of this agreement is to end tariffs on trade in the Mediterranean region by 2010.

Southwest Asian countries face both physical and political trade barriers. The lack of rivers suitable for travel transport is a major physical trade barrier for many countries in the region. Deserts also make trade extremely difficult in some countries. Mountains are also physical trade barriers in such countries as Afghanistan.

Many Southwest Asian countries specialize in the production of oil. In fact, countries in the region control about 65% of the world's oil supply. Oil from the Persian Gulf countries is exported to other countries throughout the world. This is how Gulf countries make the majority of their money. Nations such as Saudi Arabia had relatively small economies before the discovery of oil. The Persian Gulf is a huge asset to trade in the region. It provides an easily accessible route for transporting goods.

OPEC

The central organization of the world oil trade is the **Organization of Petroleum Exporting Countries (OPEC)**. OPEC is an international organization that has twelve members. The members of OPEC include the Southwest Asian countries of Iran, Iraq, Saudi Arabia, and Kuwait. OPEC's main goal is to keep the price of oil as stable as possible. If oil prices begin to fall, OPEC members usually lower their production of oil. As the supply of oil falls, the price will rise. When prices rise too quickly, OPEC nations can agree to increase production. As more oil comes on the world market, prices will fall.

OPEC holds meetings to discuss how much oil to produce. By limiting supply, they can cause the price to rise.

The 1973 Oil Embargo

Some trade barriers are political. Sometimes governments limit trade with other countries because they disagree with the actions or policies of those countries. This is a trade barrier designed to purposefully hurt the economy of another country.

The **1973 oil crisis** is one example of such a trade barrier. The 1973 oil crisis began on October 17, 1973. OPEC announced that its member nations would no longer ship oil to countries that had aided Israel in its recent war with Egypt. Those countries included the U.S. and many in Europe. OPEC raised the price of oil 70%. As a result of this embargo, the price of gasoline in the U.S. quadrupled over several months.

These actions had a large impact on industrialized nations because of their growing dependency on oil and gas. Western countries had been used to cheap and plentiful oil resources before the crisis. Oil consumption had doubled in the U.S. At the time, the U.S. was using about one-third of the world's oil.

The crisis caused the value of the American dollar to drop. It also had a widespread negative impact on the world economy. OPEC started shipping oil to Western nations again in 1974. Western economies began to get stronger again.

Wars are another type of political trade barrier. Since the 2003 invasion of Iraq, Iraqi oil production has been hampered by violence. In addition, OPEC nations have raised the price of oil. Due to this rise in price, the price of gasoline in the U.S. has increased from approximately $1.00 per gallon in 1996, to approximately $2.60 per gallon in 2009. The cost to heat homes has also risen. The average American consumer has struggled to keep up with these quickly rising prices.

Currency

Southwest Asian countries have different forms of money. The currency in Israel is the Israeli shekel. Saudi Arabian currency is the riyal. Jordan uses the dinar. Countries must have an exchange rate in order to trade with one another. The exchange rate determines how much money a currency is worth in another currency.

Some currencies have higher exchange rates than others. For example, one U.S. dollar is worth about 4 shekels. By comparison, about 3.75 Saudi riyals equal one U.S. dollar. However, a single Jordanian dinar is worth over a dollar. These exchange rates change daily.

Show What You Know

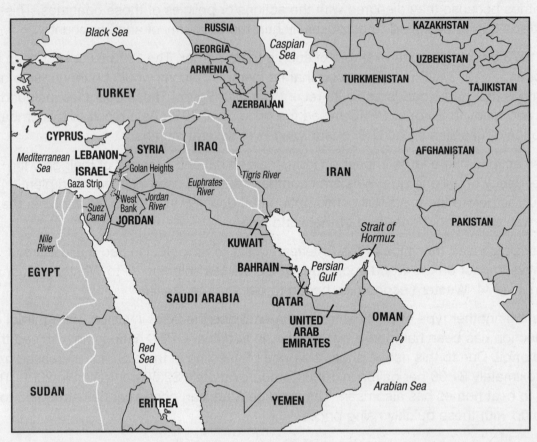

Look at the map above. What trade barriers do you see? What features do you see that might help trade?`

_____

_____

_____

_____

_____

_____

_____

_____

_____

Lesson Practice

Thinking It Through

1. The 1973 oil crisis caused all of the following EXCEPT

   A. U.S. gas prices quadrupled.

   B. the state of Israel was established.

   C. the value of the dollar dropped.

   D. many Western economies suffered.

   France's economy was hit hard by the 1973 oil crisis. The U.S. depended very heavily on imported oil at the time. Since OPEC had the power, they could control the oil prices.

2. Which of the following serves as a physical trade barrier in Southwest Asia?

   A. political tensions

   B. the Persian Gulf

   C. the Mediterranean Sea

   D. the lack of rivers

   HINT *Southwest Asia is largely an arid region of the world.*

3. The currencies of Southwest Asian countries differ. By which name is the currency of Jordan known?

   A. dinar

   B. riyal

   C. shekel

   D. dollar

4. Kuwait, Saudi Arabia, and Iran all belong to which international organization?

   A. OPEC

   B. NAFTA

   C. EU

   D. AU

25 Southwest Asian Economies

 SS7E5.c, SS7E7.a–d

There are many different types of economic systems in Southwest Asia. Most countries have mixed economies, though the amount of government control is different in each country. For the last sixty years, the region's main export has been oil. The region imports much of its food and other essential products.

Israel, Saudi Arabia, and Turkey

Israel, Saudi Arabia, and Turkey are three of the most successful economies in the region. The economic system used in each country is different.

Israel has a mixed economy that is technologically advanced. The Israeli government and private Israeli companies own and control the economy. Israel does not have many natural resources, so it must import grain, oil, military technologies, and many other goods. The country is a producer of high-tech equipment, fruit and vegetable crops, and cut diamonds. The service industry accounts for much of Israel's economy—areas such as insurance, banking, retail, and tourism account for over half of it. Israel relies heavily on U.S. economic and military aid.

Scarce water resources are used very carefully to grow crops in dry countries such as Israel.

Saudi Arabia also has a mixed economy, though the Saudi government has a lot of control over the economy. Saudi Arabia's main export is oil. The oil industry is controlled by government. This has made the Saudi royal family quite wealthy—several members of the royal family are among the richest people in the world. Oil accounts for well over half of the country's economy. Oil revenue funds the country's education, defense, transportation, health system, and housing.

In the 1900s, the Turkish government played a major role in helping its economy to grow. After World War I, the Turkish government invested large amounts of money in Turkey's weapons and steel industries. After World War II, many people objected to the Turkish government having so much control over the economy. By the 1980s, the government had begun to allow private businesses more control.

Turkey is a mixed economy today. The government still controls important industries, such as banking and communications. The number of important businesses owned and run by citizens is growing, however. Turkish companies producing clothing, automobiles, and electronics have helped the economy to grow. As in Israel, the service industry makes up about half of Turkey's economy.

Today, entrepreneurs play an important role in Turkey. The entrepreneur Aydin Dogan controls the largest oil and gas company in Turkey, as well as two television networks and two newspapers. Such entrepreneurs are new to Turkey.

Economic Growth

The economies of most Southwest Asian countries have seen many ups and downs over the years. In Israel, for example, wars have hurt the economy. Israel's gross domestic product fell during its conflict with Palestinian militants in 2001 and 2002. It has been rising since, and now stands at about $200 billion. Israel's GDP per capita—or per person—is $28,600, which is one of the highest figures in Southwest Asia.

One reason for Israel's success is that it has invested heavily in both human capital and capital resources. Israel has focused on building its agricultural industry, and has become an exporter of fruits and vegetables. The country also invests heavily in education. This helps provide skilled workers for the country's high-technology industries.

Saudi Arabia's GDP is about $575 billion, or $20,500 per person. While oil has made many Saudis rich, the government has begun encouraging the development of industries other than oil. In 1976, the Saudi government created the Saudi Basic Industries Corporation. The Saudi Basic Industries Corporation invests in capital goods. These capital goods have made the country a steady producer of steel, industrial gases, plastics, and petrochemicals.

Nearly 40% of the Saudi population is under 15 years old, which means the country will need to create many new jobs in the coming years. With this in mind, the government is increasing spending on education and training for its young people.

Iran's GDP of $850 billion is higher than any other country in the region, except Turkey. Iran's GDP per capita, however, is just $12,800. Iran's government controls most of the economy and earns money mainly from oil sales. With few thriving industries, Iran has a major problem with unemployment. Many educated young people leave the country in search of work. This may damage Iran's economy in the years ahead.

The country provides less protection for its human capital than other countries do. For example, Iran does not have private labor unions to protect workers. Iran does have a few successful entrepreneurs, however, such as N. Raisi, who founded Pak Ab Sabalan Mineral Water Co. The distribution of bottled water in the dry region is a booming enterprise.

The Role of Oil

The natural resources of a country can affect economic growth. Most Southwest Asian economies were once based on farming. When oil was discovered, it became the main source of money for many countries in the region. Governments with large oil reserves stopped investing in other parts of their economies.

Oil has made many countries wealthy. The small, oil-rich countries of Qatar and Kuwait are among the world's richest, in terms of GDP per capita. When the price of oil tumbles, however, these economies often struggle. Countries such as Turkey and Israel have built growing economies based on a more diverse group of industries.

Show What You Know

Choose a country in Southwest Asia. You are the person in charge of determining how the country should spend its money. Write a short essay explaining your choices.

_____

_____

_____

_____

_____

_____

_____

_____

_____

_____

_____

_____

_____

_____

_____

_____

_____

_____

Lesson Practice

DIRECTIONS
Circle the letter of the best answer for each item.

Thinking It Through

1. The Saudi government has encouraged the development of industries other than oil in an attempt to

   A. raise money for the royal family.

   B. encourage entrepreneurship.

   C. strengthen the country's education system.

   D. make the Saudi economy more diverse.

   The economy of Saudi Arabia is based mostly on oil. Economies based on the sale of one resource can suffer when the price of that resource falls. The Saudi government has tried to address this problem.

2. Which statement about Israel today is true?

   A. It is a pure command economy.

   B. It has a wealth of natural resources, including oil.

   C. It invests heavily in educating its people.

   D. It is not very technologically advanced.

   HINT *Israel's economy relies on a large supply of educated workers.*

3. Which statement describes the economies of many Southwest Asian countries today?

   A. They are free market economies.

   B. They are mixed economies.

   C. They are command economies.

   D. They are based on agriculture.

4. Which of the following is true of Iran's economy?

   A. It is a major importer of oil.

   B. Iran has a major problem with unemployment.

   C. The country works hard to protect its human capital.

   D. There are no entrepreneurs in Iran today.

Choose the best answer for each question. Fill in the circle in the spaces provided on your answer sheet.

1. Which of these statements BEST describes the countries that border the Persian Gulf?

    A. They all have large stores of diamonds.

    B. They all have large populations.

    C. They all have large supplies of oil.

    D. They all have epidemic disease.

2. Which phrase below defines the term "desalination"?

    A. taking salt out of salt water

    B. taking minerals out of the earth

    C. taking people out of their homelands

    D. taking oil from the ground

3. In 1973, OPEC nations refused to sell oil to the United States. This was an example of

    A. a free trade agreement.

    B. a quota.

    C. a tariff.

    D. an embargo.

4. The oldest of the three major religions of Southwest Asia is

    A. Christianity.

    B. Judaism.

    C. Islam.

    D. Buddhism.

5. The primary goal of OPEC is to

    A. keep the price of oil as stable as possible.

    B. support democracy in Southwest Asia.

    C. cause the price of oil to rise every day.

    D. lower the price of oil.

6. Which country lies partly in Southwest Asia and partly in Europe?

   A. Turkey

   B. Kuwait

   C. Saudi Arabia

   D. Iran

7. Why is the Saudi government increasing spending on education and training for its young people?

   A. The government realizes the country is running out of oil.

   B. The government wants to prepare them for future conflicts.

   C. The government wants to lower the GDP and the per capita income.

   D. The government will need to create many new jobs for them in the coming years.

8. Around the time of Jesus's death circa 33 CE, his followers started to spread his teachings. This led to the growth of which major religion?

   A. Islam

   B. Judaism

   C. Christianity

   D. Druze

9. Which of the following was NOT a factor leading to the creation of the modern state of Israel?

   A. the ancient Jewish connection to the land

   B. the Holocaust

   C. the Zionist movement

   D. the Six-Day War

10. What is one thing MOST Arabs, Kurds, and Persians have in common?

    A. Most practice Islam.

    B. Most are nomads.

    C. Arabic is the first language of all three groups.

    D. They all live in Saudi Arabia.

Use the map below to answer questions 11 and 12.

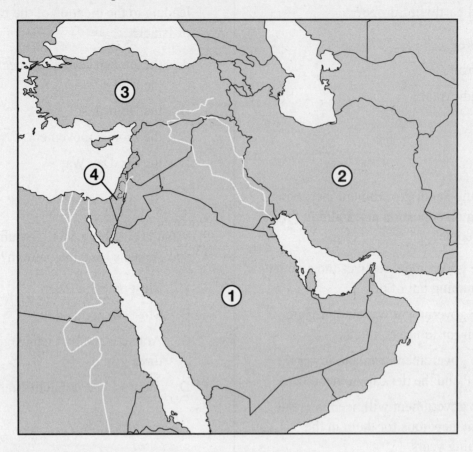

11. Which number on the map indicates the location of Iran?

   A. 1
   B. 2
   C. 3
   D. 4

12. On the map, number 1 shows the location of

   A. Saudi Arabia.
   B. Israel.
   C. Iran.
   D. Turkey.

13. Which important body of water lies between Iran and Saudi Arabia?

    A. Red Sea

    B. Euphrates River

    C. Tigris River

    D. Persian Gulf

14. The main goal of the Palestine Liberation Organization is to

    A. provide a homeland for the Jewish people.

    B. build a new state on land won in the Six-Day War.

    C. take Palestine back from the Israelis.

    D. end violence in Southwest Asia.

15. Which of the following is one of the Five Pillars of Islam?

    A. Make a hajj to Mecca at least once.

    B. Eat fish on Fridays.

    C. Eat unleavened bread during Passover.

    D. Donate one-tenth of personal income to the mosque.

16. Two large and important rivers that flow through Iraq are the

    A. Tigris and Euphrates.

    B. Nile and Congo.

    C. Jordan and Niger.

    D. Yellow and Mekong.

Use the timeline below to answer question 17.

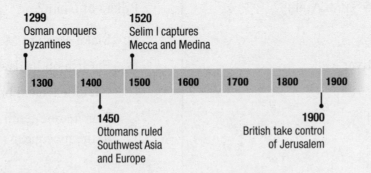

17. Which statement BEST represents the facts in the timeline?

   A. The Ottoman Empire fell within 200 years.

   B. The Ottoman Empire ruled only in Southwest Asia.

   C. The Ottoman Empire lasted 600 years.

   D. The Ottoman Empire began when the Roman Empire fell.

18. Iraq's 1990 invasion of Kuwait was the start of which international conflict?

   A. the Persian Gulf War

   B. Operation Iraqi Freedom

   C. U.S. invasion of Afghanistan

   D. Israeli-Egyptian conflict

19. One important reason for Israel's high standard of living is that

   A. Israel has the highest literacy rate in the region.

   B. Israel has huge reserves of oil and gas.

   C. Israel has not been involved in major wars.

   D. Israel is a major exporter of grain.

20. Iran's government is BEST described as

   A. a parliamentary democracy.

   B. a theocratic republic.

   C. a constitutional monarchy.

   D. a dictatorship.

21. The September 11, 2001, terrorist attacks led directly to what military action in October 2001?

   A. the U.S. invasion of Afghanistan

   B. the Persian Gulf War

   C. Operation Iraqi Freedom

   D. Israeli invasion of Lebanon

22. What is the currency of Israel?

    A. dinar

    B. shekel

    C. dollar

    D. riyal

23. Which of these countries is a parliamentary democracy?

    A. Israel

    B. Kuwait

    C. Iran

    D. Saudi Arabia

24. Which of the following statements describes the role of citizens in Saudi Arabia?

    A. All citizens 21 years of age and over may vote for national leaders.

    B. Saudi Arabia's constitution protects the rights of all citizens.

    C. Citizens select the country's king in national elections.

    D. Men can vote for some leaders, but women do not have the right to vote.

25. The economies of Israel, Turkey, and Saudi Arabia are all

    A. command economies.

    B. pure market economies.

    C. mixed economies.

    D. traditional economies.

26. The division between Shi'a and Sunni Muslims resulted from a dispute over

    A. who should control Iran.

    B. who should be Muhammad's successor.

    C. whether Muhammad is a descendant of Jesus Christ.

    D. whether or not Muslims should follow the Qur'an.

27. The countries of Southwest Asia get into disputes over water rights because

    A. the water supply in the region is very limited.

    B. Saudi Arabia controls most of the region's water.

    C. the Tigris and Euphrates rivers flow only through Iraq.

    D. there are no important rivers in the region.

28. Which of the following countries has rivers that are useful for travel, shipping, and irrigation?

A. Iran

B. Kuwait

C. Iraq

D. Afghanistan

29. What is one conflict that resulted from Europe's partitioning of the Ottoman Empire?

A. Israel demanded independence from France.

B. Germany seized control of Syria.

C. Iraqis fought for independence from Britain.

D. Saudi Arabia fought for control of Turkey.

30. How did the discovery of oil impact the economies of Southwest Asia?

A. Many economies became dependent on oil sales.

B. Countries refused to sell oil to the United States.

C. Countries decided not to produce and sell oil.

D. Saudi Arabia became the only country to exploit its oil deposits.

31. The government of Saudi Arabia has increased its spending on education and training. This is an investment in

A. human capital.

B. the stock market.

C. international commerce.

D. capital goods.

32. Turkish businessman Aydin Dogan owns oil and gas manufacturing, as well as television networks and newspapers in Turkey. Such an individual is known as

A. a nomad.

B. an entrepreneur.

C. an autocrat.

D. a legislator.

Use the list below to answer question 33.

- cultural community with common ancestry
- often shares language
- often shares traditions

33. This list describes

    A. a religious group.

    B. an ethnic group.

    C. a nationalist group.

    D. a minority group.

34. When the price of oil is low, OPEC members would MOST LIKELY

    A. refuse to sell oil.

    B. agree to lower oil production.

    C. place a higher tariff on oil.

    D. agree to raise production.

35. Which of the following may limit Iran's economic growth in the future?

    A. Iran is running out of oil.

    B. Unemployment is at an all-time low.

    C. The government no longer controls the economy.

    D. Many young, educated Iranians are leaving the country.

Use the map below to answer questions 36 and 37.

36. Israel shares borders with all of the following countries EXCEPT

    A. Saudi Arabia.

    B. Lebanon.

    C. Syria.

    D. Egypt.

37. Which of the following countries does NOT have access to the Mediterranean Sea?

    A. Lebanon

    B. Israel

    C. Jordan

    D. Syria

CHAPTER

4 Southern and Eastern Asia

26 End of Colonialism

 SS7H3.a–b

Colonialism and Nationalism

Colonialism has had a major impact on the history of Southern and Eastern Asia. Colonialism occurs when one government takes control of another, making it a colony. This includes taking control of the political, social, economic, and cultural systems of a country. The colonial power greatly benefits from the colony's resources and market, often at the expense of the people in the colony.

In many colonized countries in Southern and Eastern Asia, the citizens grew tired of the lack of control they had over their own politics, economy, and culture. In the 20th century, nationalist groups began to develop and gain power in the colonial territories. Nationalist movements are movements that seek independence for the people living in a country.

Nationalist movements eventually brought about the end of colonialism in Southern and Eastern Asia. World politics played a role as well. By the end of World War II, the social and financial drain caused by the war had weakened European colonial powers. European countries began to lose control over their colonial empires, just as nationalist movements were growing stronger. This resulted in the eventual freedom of most of the occupied countries in Asia.

Great Britain and India

British colonialism victimized India for almost 350 years. Beginning in 1600, the British completely controlled India. The British ignored Indian culture, and Indians were deprived of opportunities to succeed in their own country.

Nationalism in India took root during the 18th century. Indians educated in British schools started to wonder why they should be **westernized**, or why they should become more like the British.

There were many organizations in India that worked to achieve independence from the British. One such organization was the Indian National Congress. Its first meeting was held in Bombay (now Mumbai) in December of 1885. Surendranath Banerjea was one important leader in the Indian independence movement. He encouraged people to buy Indian-made products. He was also instrumental in the movement to boycott British-made goods.

Gandhi and Nonviolent Protest

Another important leader in the Indian independence movement was Mohandas Karamchand Gandhi. Gandhi believed in **nonviolent resistance**, a form of political protest that does not use force or violence. The goal of nonviolent resistance is to force a government to change its policies. Gandhi's movement involved massive protests, huge marches, and a full boycott on British goods, schools, and courts.

By 1920, Gandhi had established himself as the most visible leader of India's independence movement. Gandhi was arrested by the British in 1922 and spent nearly two years in prison. It took many more years of struggle, but finally on August 15, 1947, India gained its freedom from British colonial rule and became an independent nation. Gandhi's nonviolent style of protest was an inspiration to future leaders, including Nelson Mandela in South Africa and Martin Luther King Jr. in the United States.

Gandhi became one of the most famous leaders in the world. He was assassinated in Delhi in 1948.

Independence of Indochina

The French controlled the colony of Indochina, which consisted of Cambodia, Laos, and Vietnam. When World War II broke out, these colonies provided resources and labor that the French needed. The colonies felt the French government owed them independence in return for their help. The French government did not feel that Vietnam and the other colonies were ready for self-rule. The French also worried that if they left these colonies, then another imperialist nation would simply move in.

During World War II, the Japanese took over much of Southern and Eastern Asia, which included Indochina. With the Japanese defeat in WWII, the French decided to retake control of their colonies in Indochina. They soon realized, however, that a nationalist movement in Vietnam had already begun. It was headed by Ho Chi Minh, founder of the Indochina Communist Party.

The French Indochina War

Just days after Japan's surrender in August 1945, Vietnamese nationalist soldiers moved into the capital city of Hanoi, in northern Vietnam. On September 2, in front of a massive crowd, Ho Chi Minh declared Vietnam's independence.

Unwilling to surrender its former colony, France sent its own soldiers to Vietnam. The soldiers landed in the southern city of Saigon and soon took control of the southern half of the country. By 1946, Ho Chi Mihn's forces were at war with the French, a long conflict that became known as the French Indochina War. Under Ho Chi Minh's leadership, Communist fighters finally defeated the French at Dien Bien Phu on May 7, 1954. France was forced to recognize Vietnam's independence.

During these years, Cambodia and Laos achieved independence from France as well. By the time the Vietnamese defeated France in 1954, France had lost its entire colony in Indochina.

Show What You Know

In the space below, create a timeline of key events from the independence movements in India and Vietnam.

Lesson Practice

DIRECTIONS
Circle the letter of the best answer for each item.

Thinking It Through

1. Which statement is true about the relationship between Great Britain and India?

    A. India gained its independence before World War II ended.

    B. India gained its independence after World War II.

    C. France gave India its independence.

    D. India remains one of Great Britain's colonies to this day.

It took a long time for India to gain its independence. It achieved independence at about the same time as many other colonies.

2. A major force behind many independence movements was

    A. the Sepoy Rebellion.

    B. the East India Company.

    C. nationalism.

    D. Marxism.

    HINT *People had a strong devotion to their countries, and they wanted political independence.*

3. Mohandas K. Gandhi supported a strategy of

    A. colonialism.

    B. guerrilla warfare.

    C. nonviolent protest.

    D. terrorism.

4. A major leader in Vietnam's independence movement was

    A. Mohandas K. Gandhi.

    B. Surendranath Banerjea.

    C. Prince Norodom Sihanouk.

    D. Ho Chi Minh.

27 Japan After World War II

 SS7H3.c

World War II was fought in two main theaters: the European Theater and the Pacific Theater. So much fighting took place in Asia that many Asian countries needed to be rebuilt after the war. Prior to and during World War II, Japan had taken over parts of China and Korea and other areas of Southern and Eastern Asia.

Japan After World War II

Japan was among the countries most heavily damaged by the war. American planes bombed Japanese cities, leaving many of them in ruins. In August 1945, the United States dropped atomic bombs on two Japanese cities, Hiroshima and Nagasaki. The Japanese finally admitted defeat. Aboard the *U.S.S. Missouri* in Tokyo Harbor on September 2, 1945, Japan signed an official surrender. Japan was now under the control of a U.S. Army occupation led by General Douglas MacArthur.

An aerial view of the bombings of Japan

The U.S. Role in Rebuilding

At the end of the war, much of Japan's infrastructure was gone. **Infrastructure** consists of the public systems and services of a nation. The atomic bombs, as well as the regular bombs of war, were responsible for the destruction.

U.S. leaders wanted Japan to become a peaceful nation, with a stable government that was chosen by its citizens. The U.S. believed that the social, political, and economic conditions that allowed for the extremely militaristic colonial empire of Japan to exist had to be destroyed.

The United States and other world powers had another goal in mind as well. Japan had caused the war in the Pacific, which began with the Japanese attack on the American naval base at Pearl Harbor, Hawaii, in December 1941. When the war finally ended, leading world powers wanted to make sure that Japan never became a strong military power again.

Under the leadership of General MacArthur, the United States began the enormous job of helping Japan to rebuild. The U.S. helped Japan strengthen its economy by helping to rebuild transportation systems, industry, and urban infrastructure. In the countryside, a land reform program was put in place. Poor farmers, who had never owned their own land, were given small plots of land. Farm productivity increased quickly. Labor unions were encouraged, while those business leaders who were a major part of the militaristic Japan of World War II were stripped of their power.

Japan could keep its home islands but had to give up control of all of its overseas possessions. Manchuria once again became a part of China. Japan could no longer claim Formosa (now called Taiwan). The Soviet Union occupied southern Sakhalin and the Kurile islands to the north. The United States controlled the Ryukyu, Bonin, and Volcano islands to the south.

Many Japanese cities, including the capital city of Tokyo, were left in ruins when the war ended.

A New Constitution

One of the major goals of the U.S. rebuilding effort in Japan was to change the way Japan was ruled. MacArthur did not wish to force the Japanese to adopt a particular style of government. But it was the U.S. policy to help Japan establish a democratic government, with active citizen participation and laws protecting people's basic rights and freedoms.

On May 3, 1947, Japan's new constitution became official. Under this constitution, the Japanese emperor was stripped of his power and became a figurehead. An elected legislature was given important powers. The new law also included a bill of rights. Article 9 of the document states that Japan would never again be the aggressor in war. Japan could no longer use its land, sea, or air forces to settle international disputes. The new constitution had strong support among the people of Japan.

The U.S. occupation of Japan lasted from 1945 to 1952. On April 28, 1952, Japan became a fully sovereign nation again. In general, the Japanese people were comfortable with the changes that took place after World War II. The economy recovered quickly and grew rapidly in the decades ahead. Today, Japan has the third-largest economy in the world, following only China and the United States.

Show What You Know

Prior to and during World War II, Japan had taken over parts of China as well as Korea and other areas of Southern and Eastern Asia. After World War II, the United States took over Japan until it was rebuilt both economically and politically. Why does the takeover of Japan by the United States seem more acceptable than Japan's taking over Korea and China?

_____

_____

_____

_____

_____

_____

_____

_____

_____

_____

_____

_____

_____

_____

_____

_____

_____

_____

_____

_____

_____

_____

Lesson Practice

DIRECTIONS
Circle the letter of the best answer for each item.

Thinking It Through

1. Which statement about Japan today is true?

   A. Japan is controlled by an army of occupation.

   B. Japan controls the same amount of land as during World War II.

   C. Japan is a sovereign nation.

   D. Japan refuses to have diplomatic relations with China.

After World War II, certain plans were put in place in Japan to prevent it from ever becoming a militaristic nation again and to help Japan create a government and economy that could stand on its own.

2. All of the following were goals of the United States' rebuilding effort in Japan EXCEPT

   A. rebuilding Japan's infrastructure.

   B. establishing a new, democratic government.

   C. rebuilding Japan's military strength.

   D. helping Japan's economy recover.

   HINT *U.S. leaders blamed Japan's military for the war in the Pacific and wanted to make sure Japan would not start additional wars in the future.*

3. The American general who was in charge of the U.S. army of occupation in Japan was

   A. Douglas MacArthur.

   B. Dwight Eisenhower.

   C. George Patton.

   D. Omar Bradley.

4. Which of the following was true of the constitution that went into effect in Japan in 1947?

   A. Japan became an autocratic state.

   B. Japan's emperor was left with only symbolic powers.

   C. Japan adopted a new, planned economy.

   D. The elected legislature was abolished.

28 The Reign of Mao Zedong

 SS7H3.d

The Reign of Mao Zedong

The Chinese leader Mao Zedong remains controversial. Some argue that his programs brought improvements to China, such as making women more equal to men and increasing education for the masses. Others say that he is responsible for the deaths of millions of Chinese and that he sent China backward economically, culturally, and politically.

The Rise of Mao

Mao Zedong came from a peasant background. He was educated at Hunan Teacher's College. In 1918, he got a job in the library at Beijing University. He studied Marxist writings with Beijing University's head librarian, Li Dazhao. **Marxism** is a political philosophy that focuses on class struggle. In Marxism, the workers would cause the revolution; the eventual goal is to have a classless society where all people are equal. Many basic ideas of communism come out of Marxist philosophy.

In the early 20th century, two very different political parties were fighting for power in China—the Kuomintang (KMT) and the Chinese Communist Party (CCP). The KMT wanted a republic and favored capitalism. The CCP favored a command economy based on Marxism.

In 1921, Mao attended the founding meeting of the Chinese Communist Party in Shanghai. In 1923, while keeping his CCP membership, Mao joined the Kuomintang, because together the KMT and CCP were fighting against ruling warlords in China. A couple of years after the KMT's leader, Sun Yat-sen (or Sun Yixian), died in 1925, the KMT and CCP alliance ended. The new KMT leader, Chiang Kai-shek (or Jiang Jieshi), attempted to wipe out the Communists.

The Long March

In 1934, Chiang's 700,000 troops surrounded Mao's Red Army troops in Jiangxi province in the south. Mao and his 100,000 Communists (the Red Army) fled Chiang's blockade. The Communists began their extremely dangerous journey called the **Long March**. They marched 6,000 miles to Yan'an, in northern China. Much of the march was through swampland and over mountains.

Along the way, they attended a CCP meeting at Zunyi. Years earlier, Mao had been criticized for his ideas about how communism would work in China. Now though, he and his supporters found favor with many CCP members. After about a year on the Long March, Mao and his 6,000–7,000 survivors settled in the caves of Yan'an. Mao continued to gain more followers.

Chinese peasants marching

China during World War II

In the years before World War II, Japan invaded Manchuria, which is located in northeastern China. The Japanese set up a government known as a **puppet state**. This is a government set up in a nation that is actually run buy an outside nation. In Manchuria, a Chinese leader was the head of the government, but the Japanese government made all of the decisions. In 1937, Japan invaded China, and until Japan surrendered at the end of World War II, Japanese forces remained in China.

During the war, members of Mao's CCP worked with the KMT to try to remove the Japanese from China. Chinese of all political beliefs were thrilled when the Japanese surrendered on September 2, 1945. Many problems remained in the nation of China, though. The opposing viewpoints of the KMT and CCP left China on the brink of civil war. China needed to be reunified under one government. Furthermore, years of fighting with the Japanese had left China devastated. It needed to be reconstructed.

Economically, China was in trouble as well. Inflation was out of control. The Chinese government had to import huge amounts of grain and cotton. Excessive trading regulations and corrupt practices further contributed to the poor Chinese economy. International aid was not enough to take care of the needs of the Chinese people after World War II.

The Communists Win

U.S. troops assisted China once World War II ended. U.S. General Douglas MacArthur required that Japanese forces surrender to the Nationalists (KMT). Yet, the Chinese Communist forces continued to gain strength in China. Both the CCP and KMT wanted control of Manchuria, an area rich in natural resources and important to control for strategic geographic reasons. Civil war broke out yet again in China, and the KMT and CCP fought against each other until 1949.

In the end, Mao's peasant support and Red Army defeated the KMT. In Tiananmen Square, in China's capital, Beijing, on October 1, 1949, Mao established the People's Republic of China. Mao became the chairman of the CCP. He is still referred to as Chairman Mao.

A Great Leap Forward?

In 1958, Mao instituted the **Great Leap Forward**. This was a series of policies that Mao thought would help China to become equal to the leading powers of the West in agricultural and industrial production. Mao believed in the power of the peasants to bring about great results. Unfortunately, the peasants' labor was not enough to bring about the results Mao desired. Sometimes peasants even lied about the amount of grain that had been produced rather than disappoint their leader. Instead of success, massive famine resulted. Millions of people died throughout China.

The Cultural Revolution

Several actions led up to the official start of China's **Cultural Revolution** on June 1, 1966. Mao realized that a large gap still existed between the educated elite of the cities and the peasants of the countryside. Mao thought that through the Cultural Revolution, he could renew the spirit of the Chinese revolution.

Mao Zedong

Mao's supporters started to write articles and editorials, and began to create posters speaking out against the bourgeoisie of Chinese society. The **bourgeoisie** are often landowners or factory owners who have power over the working class and peasants. Though some leaders in China thought economic and political reforms should slow down, Mao thought more radical measures needed to be taken.

Mao placed key people in positions of power to help him carry out the Cultural Revolution. Jiang Qing, Mao's wife, controlled the culture of Chinese society. She encouraged the creation of plays and art that glorified Mao. Lin Biao, defense minister, kept the military in line. Chen Boda, Kang Sheng, and Wang Dongxing carried out directives about ideas and security. Zhou Enlai, premier of China, made sure that the country kept running. Interestingly, many of these top leaders would turn against one another at various times during the Cultural Revolution.

Mao encouraged high school students to form groups called Red Guards. These Red Guards were given much power and mistreated many innocent people. Foreign ideas and old Chinese cultural ideas were frowned upon. The Red Guards had the government's permission to smash and destroy books, artwork, religious temples, or anything else that showed connections to China's past or to foreign ideas.

Schools and universities were closed. Teachers were mistreated and often sent out to the countryside to do hard labor. Artists, writers, as well as anyone with connections to foreigners, were publicly criticized. Family members were often separated for years. They were sent off to work doing manual labor out in the countryside. Neighbors accused one another for "crimes" that they may or may not have committed. No one was safe.

The Cultural Revolution was a time of great chaos in China. Throughout this period, many innocent people were killed or committed suicide. It lasted for a total of ten years and only ended when Mao died in 1976.

Reforms and Tiananmen Square

After the death of Mao, leaders decided to focus on achieving faster economic growth. Reformers led by Deng Xiaoping allowed the Chinese people a bit more freedom than they had under Mao. Millions were released from labor camps, and fewer people were jailed for criticizing the government.

The reformers worked to improve relations with the United States, and China opened its economy more to international trade. In both the countryside and cities, people were given more economic freedom.

These reforms were welcomed by the Chinese people, though many believed change was happening too slowly. As China became more open to the outside world, people could see the better conditions and greater freedoms allowed in other countries. They wanted faster change at home. Students led a growing protest movement in the late 1980s. In cities across the country, crowds gathered to demand more political and economic freedom.

In April 1989, tens of thousands of protestors gathered in Tiananmen Square in the capital city of Beijing. Government leaders warned the protesters to leave, but the crowds continued to grow. Soon the protestors numbered about one million.

Chinese leaders used violence to end massive protests in Tiananmen Square in 1989.

Alarmed by the size of the public protests, the government decided to crack down. On the night of June 3, tanks rolled into Tiananmen Square. Heavily armed soldiers fired into the crowd, while tanks crushed protestors. Thousands more were arrested and sent to prison, and some were executed. The Chinese government has since tried to hide details of the incident, but it is known that hundreds of protestors were killed and thousands more injured.

Show What You Know

A political cartoon takes an event and uses humor to get a point across about the event. It may use a few words and often uses exaggerated drawings. In the space provided, create a political cartoon that makes a point about one of the events that occurred under Mao Zedong's rule of China.

Lesson Practice

DIRECTIONS
Circle the letter of the best answer for each item.

Thinking It Through

1. Which program of Mao's was supposed to make China more equal economically with leading nations of the world?

   A. Cultural Revolution

   B. Great Leap Forward

   C. Long March

   D. KMT and CCP unification

   This was a series of policies that were supposed to make China more agriculturally and industrially equal to other powerful nations of the world. These policies were supposed to have very quick, positive effects.

2. How would you describe the relationship of the Kuomintang (KMT) and the Chinese Communist Party (CCP)?

   A. They are active political parties in the nation of Korea.

   B. They sometimes worked together to fight against a common enemy.

   C. They never worked together for the good of the Chinese country.

   D. They have similar political views about how China should be run.

   HINT *These two political parties could sometimes put their differences aside for the good of China.*

3. Which political party won the civil war in China and established the People's Republic of China on October 1, 1949?

   A. Bourgeoisie

   B. Marxists

   C. KMT

   D. CCP

4. The Chinese government's response to the Tiananmen Square protests in 1989 was to

   A. agree to greater economic freedoms.

   B. negotiate with the protestors.

   C. use military force to destroy the protests.

   D. agree to greater political freedoms.

29 The Korean War

 SS7H3.e

Background Information

Korea is located in northeast Asia and shares a border with China. In 1910, Japan took over Korea as a colony and ruled it for 35 years. Japan tried to suppress Korea's culture and language, just as other colonial powers had done in their colonies.

Following World War II, Japanese control over Korea was replaced by Soviet and American presence that split the country into two roughly equal parts at the **38th parallel**. This border divided the separate countries of Communist North Korea and democratic South Korea. Kim Il-sung became North Korea's first leader. The new government adopted the political structure of the Soviet Union. Syngman Rhee became president of South Korea.

The Cold War

The division of Korea took place just as the Cold War was getting started. The **Cold War** was a struggle for world power between the United States and the Soviet Union. It was called the Cold War because there was no actual warfare between the Soviet Union and the United States. Instead, the two superpowers supported armed conflicts between democratic and Communist nations around the world. The first of these conflicts happened in Korea.

A common theory of the time was the **domino theory**. It was believed that if one nation fell to communism, then others in the area would follow just like dominoes falling over. The United States feared that if all of Korea became a Communist nation, then other nations in Asia would become Communist as well.

A Back-and-Forth War

On June 25, 1950, Communist forces from North Korea invaded South Korea. North Korea wanted to unite all of Korea under Communist rule. In less than a week, the capital of South Korea, Seoul, fell to North Korean forces. The United Nations and the United States sided with South Korea.

By August of 1950, South Korean and U.S. troops, organized under the United Nations, had withdrawn to the Pusan Perimeter in the south. By the end of August, all UN forces (which were mostly American, but also came from countries such as Ethiopia, Turkey, Britain, France, and the Philippines) were in the Pusan Perimeter.

During September of 1950, U.S. and Korean troops captured Inchon. Inchon was a key area to control. It is on the coast of South Korea and west of Seoul. Shortly after taking Inchon, U.S. forces got control of Seoul. It seemed as if victory was in reach. By October, UN forces captured Pyongyang, the capital of North Korea.

The United States did not think that the Chinese would help the North Koreans, but they did. By the end of October 1950, the Chinese army started attacking UN forces in North Korea. On January 4, 1951, the Chinese captured Seoul. By March, a UN counteroffensive retook Seoul. U.S. President Harry S. Truman made a bold decision in April of 1951. Truman dismissed General Douglas MacArthur because of the general's insubordination and unwillingness to conduct a limited war.

Final Two Years of the War

In June 1951, the second phase of the Korean War started. It would last for two years. Massive artillery fights around the 38th parallel took place. Many infantry struggled over a few hills or just thousands of yards of terrain. During this period, peace negotiations took place without much hope of ending the war.

From July to August 1952, U.S. air strikes almost destroyed Pyongyang. The Korean War was the first time jets were used to fight in a war. On October 8, 1952, peace talks reached a deadlock, and the sides involved took a break. Talks resumed on March 30, 1953. On July 27, 1953, an agreement was signed in Panmunjom, along the 38th parallel. This agreement continued the division of Korea at this parallel.

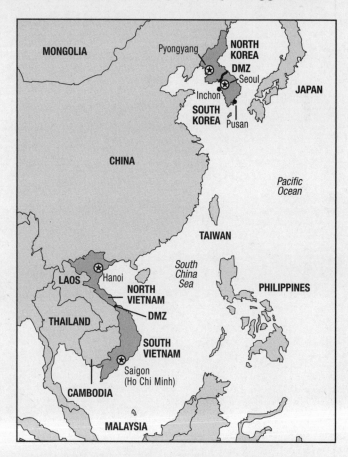

Results of the War

The war lasted three years and ended in a **stalemate**, with neither side gaining much in terms of territory. In 1953, an armistice was declared. An **armistice** is an agreement to stop fighting. No peace treaty ending the war has ever been signed. The 38th parallel remains the approximate border between North and South Korea with a **demilitarized zone (DMZ)** in between the two countries. Today, roughly 38,000 United States soldiers provide a defense force guarding against invasion from the militant North Koreans. South Korea has become a prosperous country embracing democratic ideals. North Korea remains a Communist-led country that has suffered many economic problems over the years. About three million people died from starvation there in the second half of the 1990s. The Korean War was the first instance of armed conflict between democratic nations and the Communist Bloc. The armistice that ended the Korean War remains the longest cease-fire in modern military history.

Show What You Know

In the space provided, sketch a simple map of the two Koreas. Use the map on page 187 to help you. Draw a line roughly where the 38th parallel should be and label it as the demilitarized zone (DMZ). Label North Korea and its capital. Label South Korea and its capital. Identify other key places where fighting occurred during the Korean War, such as Inchon and Pusan.

Lesson Practice

Thinking It Through

1. What does the 38th parallel do?

   This area was created after World War II. It is symbolic of the Cold War because of what it does.

   A. It separates North Korea from South Korea.

   B. It marks the area where Soviet troops are stationed.

   C. It indicates the northernmost border of North Korea.

   D. It surrounds the Pusan Perimeter.

2. The Korean War started when

   A. North Korean forces invaded South Korea.

   B. South Korean forces invaded North Korea.

   C. the Soviet Union invaded South Korea.

   D. the United States invaded North Korea.

   HINT *One nation wanted to take over all of Korea to make it Communist.*

3. The main U.S. goal in the Korean War was to

   A. support the North Korean government.

   B. gain territory in China.

   C. unite the country under Kim Il-sung.

   D. stop the spread of communism.

4. What happened to U.S. General Douglas MacArthur during the Korean War?

   A. He became a hero to North Koreans.

   B. President Truman fired him.

   C. The American people disgraced him.

   D. He got transferred to China.

30 The Vietnam War

 SS7H3.e

Vietnam is a country in Southern Asia, located south of China, east of Cambodia and Laos, with the South China Sea to its east. In 1940, Japan occupied the northern part of Vietnam and then the rest of Indochina the following year. Indochina was largely unaffected by the Japanese occupation. After World War II, the Japanese were forced to leave Southern and Eastern Asia. The French saw this as their chance to reclaim Indochina—the present-day nations of Vietnam, Laos, and Cambodia. The Vietnamese, however, wanted self-rule for their country.

The French Indochina War began. Ho Chi Minh and his **Viet Minh**, the nationalist and Communist forces in Vietnam, defeated the French in 1954. However, war in Vietnam continued until 1975.

Causes of the Vietnam War

Once the Vietnamese defeated the French, an international peace conference was held in Geneva. It was decided that Vietnam would be divided at 17° N latitude (17th parallel). North of this line, Ho Chi Minh and his Communist forces would run the government. North Vietnam's capital was in Hanoi. In the south, the non-Communist government of President Ngo Dinh Diem was in control. South Vietnam's capital was in Saigon.

Rice paddy

The two countries were separated by a demilitarized zone similar to that of Korea. Communist North Vietnam was supported by both the Soviet Union and China. The United States and its allies supported South Vietnam. The Vietnam War was primarily a civil war involving the North Vietnamese Communists and the South Vietnamese Viet Cong fighting against others in South Vietnam. The **Viet Cong** were Communists seeking reunification of the country under Communist rule. The United States viewed the conflict as another example of Communist aggression.

Just as in the Korean War, the domino theory played a part in the Vietnam War. U.S. President Dwight Eisenhower believed that if Vietnam fell to communism, then other nations in the region would, too. Therefore, President Eisenhower felt the U.S. presence in Vietnam was needed in order to prevent the Communists from overtaking all of Vietnam.

The Viet Cong, Communist **guerillas** based in South Vietnam, gained more and more strength when Diem ruled as a dictator. Guerillas used hit-and-run tactics when fighting rather than traditional fighting methods. Since the Communists continued to gain strength throughout all of Vietnam, the United States decided to increase its presence.

U.S. Involvement
The war escalated with the Gulf of Tonkin incident in 1964, when it was said that the North Vietnamese attacked U.S. Navy ships. As a result of the Gulf of Tonkin incident, President Lyndon Johnson received support from the U.S. Congress to increase U.S. involvement in the war. In 1965, U.S. combat troops were sent to Vietnam.

Effective Strategies of the Vietnamese
Long before U.S. involvement increased in Vietnam, North Vietnamese troops started using the **Ho Chi Minh Trail**. This was a system of paths through the jungles and mountains that connected North Vietnam to South Vietnam via Laos and Cambodia. During the 1960s, the paths and traffic on the trail increased despite U.S. bombing raids aimed at lessening its effectiveness. It took over one month to get from North to South Vietnam using the Ho Chi Minh Trail, yet it was a very effective part of the Vietnam War.

The Communists launched the Tet Offensive in 1968. It did not succeed in capturing the main cities of South Vietnam as it was intended to, but it did succeed in reducing the American public's support of the war. After the Tet Offensive, President Richard Nixon would begin to withdraw U.S. troops from Vietnam. This policy of turning over control of the war to South Vietnam while the U.S. troops withdrew was called **Vietnamization**. The last U.S. troops in Vietnam left in 1973, after the signing of the Paris Peace Accords.

A U.S. helicopter in Vietnam

Results of the War
The Vietnam War showed the world that even the United States, with the most advanced army and the best equipment, could be defeated by a lesser power. The Viet Cong's guerilla tactics worked, and the more the U.S. bombed the Vietnamese countryside, the more the local people sided with the Viet Cong.

The Vietnam War involved armed conflicts in Vietnam's neighboring countries of Cambodia and Laos, too. The U.S. bombed both of these countries to try to destroy the Viet Cong's hiding places, as well as the Ho Chi Minh Trail. The Vietnam War resulted in over 58,000 U.S. deaths and about 2 million Vietnamese deaths. U.S. involvement in the war lasted through the terms of four presidents—Dwight Eisenhower, John F. Kennedy, Lyndon Johnson, and Richard Nixon.

This was the first time in American history that the public was so clearly against war. The Vietnam War was unpopular in the United States because of the large number of U.S. casualties and the draft of males into the armed forces. The dissent ultimately caused President Johnson to withdraw from the 1968 presidential election.

The war ended in 1975, when the South Vietnamese surrendered before the capture of Saigon by the North Vietnamese army. In 1976, North Vietnam united both North and South Vietnam to form the Socialist Republic of Vietnam. Saigon was renamed Ho Chi Minh City in honor of the former president of North Vietnam. Hanoi became the country's capital. Vietnam remains a Communist country to this day.

Show What You Know

Write about the main reasons why the Viet Cong and North Vietnamese forces were able to defeat a much more powerful and advanced American army.

_____

_____

_____

_____

_____

_____

_____

_____

_____

_____

_____

_____

_____

_____

_____

_____

_____

Lesson Practice

Circle the letter of the best answer for each item.

Thinking It Through

1. After the Tet Offensive, President Nixon started to withdraw U.S. troops because

   A. he wanted the South Vietnamese to take a more active role in combat.

   B. he wanted the North Vietnamese to take a more active role in combat.

   C. he wanted the troops to spend more time trying to destroy the Ho Chi Minh Trail.

   D. he needed to send the troops to another war.

As a result of the American public's outcry against the war, Nixon felt some changes needed to be made regarding America's role in the war.

2. Who was Ho Chi Minh?

   A. the leader of South Vietnam throughout the war

   B. the leader of North Vietnam throughout the war

   C. a soldier captured by the Americans and tried as a war criminal

   D. a leader who only had followers in North Vietnam during the war

   HINT *Ho Chi Minh had followers throughout the nation.*

3. Which two nations were directly affected by U.S. actions in the Vietnam War?

   A. Indonesia and Australia

   B. Cambodia and Australia

   C. Laos and Thailand

   D. Laos and Cambodia

4. At the end of the Vietnam War, who was victorious?

   A. the Americans

   B. the South Koreans

   C. the Communists

   D. the Chinese

31 Physical Features of Southern and Eastern Asia

 SS7G9.a–b, SS7G11.a–b

Oceans, seas, and bays play an important role in the lives of Asians. Japan is called an **archipelago**, a chain of islands. Japan's main island is called Honshu. The Himalayan Mountains and Gobi Desert are other natural features located in eastern Asia.

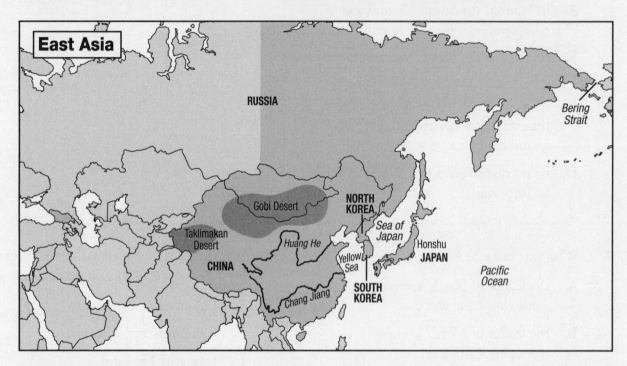

Impact of Location on Trade, Agriculture, and Industry

A large area of India's coast is surrounded by water. Trading ships have reached India's coast for centuries. In modern times, technology has allowed India to easily connect with other nations, especially for business purposes. India has one of the largest economies in the world. Within Asia, India's economy is behind only Japan's and China's. Services, such as call centers and tourism, in India's economy account for 61% of its gross domestic product (GDP). The GDP is the market value of all of the goods and services a country produces. Industry accounts for 19% of India's GDP. Agriculture accounts for 20% of India's GDP. A large portion of India's population, almost two-thirds, works in the agriculture sector.

Pakistan shares a long border with India. It is a somewhat young nation compared to India. Pakistan was created out of India when India got its independence from Great Britain in 1947. Most of the Indus River falls within Pakistan, and Pakistan's population is concentrated mostly in the Indus Valley region.

Pakistan's workforce is divided up as follows: 42% in agriculture, 38% in public services (government jobs), and 20% in industry. Regarding international trade, Pakistan exports $14.85 billion in goods and imports $21.26 billion. Most of its goods are exported to the United States. Most of its imports come from China.

Indonesia is made up of more than 17,000 islands, but people live on only 6,000 of them. Indonesia's workforce includes the following: 46.1% in agriculture, 18.5% in trade and restaurants, 12% in manufacturing, and 10.7% in public services. In 2005, Indonesia exported $85.6 billion worth of goods to their major markets in Japan, the United States, Singapore, China, and the European Union. That year, Indonesia imported $57.5 billion worth of goods from Japan, China, the U.S., Thailand, and the EU.

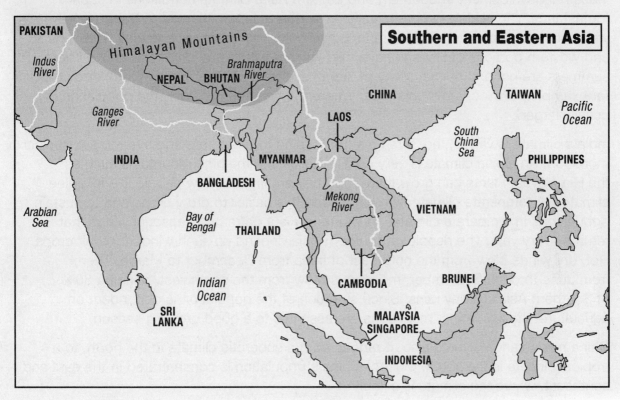

China has a large land mass. Agriculture and forestry account for 50% of the work force, and 23% of the workforce is in industry and commerce. Even though about 50% of the workforce is involved in agricultural production, only about 10% of China's land is suitable for cultivation. Nonetheless, China is still one of the largest producers of rice in the world.

Simply because of its geography, Japan's workforce is much different from the other nations discussed. Japan's work force is as follows: 42% in public services; 46% in trade, manufacturing, mining, and construction; 5% in agriculture, forestry, and fisheries, and 3% in government. Japan puts many protections and subsidies in place to help the agriculture sector of its economy. Only 15% of Japan's land can grow crops, so farmers work hard to produce the most crops per hectare (about two and a half acres). Japan's crop yields are some of the highest in the world.

The Effects of Climate

Climatic conditions have had a major effect on population distribution, agriculture, and industrial development in Southern and Eastern Asia. Climate conditions in Japan, for instance, vary widely geographically. In northern Japan, the city of Sapporo has warm summers, but the winters are long and cold, with plenty of snowfall. The central and western portions of Honshu have mild winters without much or any snow. There, summers are hot and humid. Many of Japan's largest cities—Tokyo, Kyoto, and Osaka, for example—are located in this area. Where the weather is milder, the population is usually larger.

India's climate is varied, too. It ranges from alpine to temperate and even to subtropical monsoon. An alpine climate is very cold and exists in the high mountains such as the Himalayas. Plants can grow there, but they are limited. Few people live in alpine climates. A temperate climate is much milder. It is easier to grow crops and to sustain populations in temperate climates. A **monsoon** is a pattern of seasonal winds that returns every year. The people of Southern Asia depend on such winds for their crops. Hot, dry winds blow from the northeast of India from December to March. Then, from June through September, monsoons blow from the southwest, bringing 80% of Southern Asia's yearly rains. Since so much of the population is dependent on agriculture, these summer monsoons are essential to a good growing season.

China has a varied climate also. It ranges from a subarctic climate in the north, to a tropical climate in the south. Most of China's population is concentrated in the east and southeast, where the climate is milder.

Distribution of Natural Resources

Throughout Asia, natural resources are unevenly distributed. A lack of natural resources does not mean that a country cannot be prosperous, however.

Japan has few natural resources, but the Japanese use their trade to get the funds that they need to purchase raw materials. They then use these raw materials to produce goods to sell in the international market. With this strategy, Japan has become an economic powerhouse. Even the resources that Japan does have in abundance, like its coastal waters that provide fish and other marine life, are not enough for Japanese demand. The Japanese, therefore, supplement their fish needs with fish caught in distant waters and with imported fish.

Bangladesh's natural resources include fertile soil, water, and natural gas. Bangladesh has a high population because of its fertile soil, but it is also susceptible to flooding, tornadoes, and cyclones. Despite its natural resources, it is one of the world's poorest nations.

India has plentiful natural resources including coal, iron ore, diamonds, crude oil, and a variety of minerals and metals. It has a large population, second only to the population of China. The middle class in India is large and continues to grow. There is, however, a large portion (28%) of India's population that lives below the poverty line.

China's natural resources include coal, iron ore, crude oil, a variety of minerals and metals, and the potential for the world's largest source of hydropower. China produces the most coal of any country in the world, but it also consumes the most. Despite its abundant natural resources, China was a poor nation for many years. With economic reforms of the 1980s came increased agricultural and industrial output. China produces all of the grain that its country now needs. Since economic reforms were put in place, China's economy has had ups and downs, but in more recent years, the economy has grown at about 10% per year. This is among the highest growth rates in the world. When natural resources are paired with sound economic policies, the result can be beneficial.

Overall Effects of Geography

In general, geography affects where people live, what they do there, and how they move around. The Indo-Gangetic Plain offers an example to demonstrate this.

This large plain in India lies between the Himalayan mountain ranges and the Deccan Plateau. Much of this area benefits from the three large rivers of Southern Asia: the Ganges, the Indus, and the Brahmaputra. All three have their sources in the Himalayas. From the mountains, these rivers carry silt which fertilizes farmland on the plains. These rivers also provide a reliable source of irrigation. As a result of its steady source of water, its fertile soil, and its long growing season, the Indo-Gangetic Plain is densely populated. Throughout this region, farmers raise rice, wheat, and jute.

Transportation in the Indo-Gangetic Plain area is easier than in mountainous areas. The land is relatively level, so it is possible to build and maintain roads. The rivers among the plains can be used for transportation, too.

In mountainous areas, travel is much more difficult. Mountain passes are important because they allow people to travel through or over the mountains. The Khyber Pass has been used for centuries, and has been the way that invading armies took over Southern Asia from the northwest. Presently, the Khyber Pass connects Afghanistan to Pakistan.

Show What You Know

Write about some geographic features that most likely help nations become successful.

_____

_____

_____

_____

_____

_____

_____

_____

_____

_____

_____

_____

_____

_____

_____

_____

_____

_____

_____

_____

_____

_____

_____

_____

_____

_____

_____

Lesson Practice

DIRECTIONS
Circle the letter of the best answer for each item.

Thinking It Through

1. Many people in India depend upon which geographic feature for their livelihood?

   A. rivers

   B. monsoons

   C. mountains

   D. coastlines

   This geographic feature controls rainfall. Almost two-thirds of India's workforce works in the agriculture sector.

2. In Japan, the LEAST amount of people work in which sector?

   A. service

   B. manufacturing

   C. trade

   D. agriculture

   HINT *Japan has a limited amount of natural resources and land.*

3. MOST of China's population is concentrated in the

   A. east and southeast.

   B. south.

   C. west.

   D. north and northwest.

4. The nation that is located on the Bay of Bengal and has very fertile soil is

   A. Bangladesh.

   B. Pakistan.

   C. Vietnam.

   D. China.

32 Southern and Eastern Asian Environmental Policies

SS7G10.a–b

Asia covers about one-third of the world's land area, but it is home to three-fifths of the world's population. Two Asian nations—India and China—have by far the largest populations in the world. With well over one billion people in each country, India and China are home to about 40% of the people in the world. This huge and growing population puts pressure on the environment of Asia. Producing enough food and other goods for all of Asia's people requires the use of tremendous amounts of natural resources. This is the cause of many serious environmental challenges in the 21st century.

River Pollution

The pollution of India's Ganges River is an example of the type of environmental damage facing India today. About 400 million people live along the Ganges. Factories and farms also line the long river, and all this activity causes pollution. Garbage and human waste flows into the river, along with artificial fertilizers used on crops and pollution from factories. The polluted water of the Ganges causes serious health problems for many people living along the river.

The Yangtze River is the longest river in China and the third-longest in the world. It is considered the most important river in China because it flows through China's most fertile land. Water from the Yangtze is used to produce about half of all the food grown in China. This makes pollution in the Yangtze very dangerous. Since China began its rapid industrial growth in the second half of the 20th century, large amounts of waste from factories have flowed into the river. Sewage is also a major cause of water pollution. Polluted river water spreads disease and also threatens the survival of rare species, including the Yangtze River dolphin.

Air Pollution

Air pollution is also a large problem in many Asian nations. The rapidly growing number of cars and trucks on Asian roads is one major cause of air pollution. Factories and power plants that burn coal and other fossil fuels are another major cause. An additional challenge in India is that there are many small industrial workshops. Because of this, it is difficult for the government to enforce laws to improve air pollution.

Air pollution in Beijing can cause health problems for the city's residents.

Air pollution causes sickness and many deaths every year. According to a World Bank report, twelve of the fifteen most polluted cities in the world are in China and

India—eight in China and four in India. Deaths from urban air pollution in China and India are among the highest in the world.

China's polluted air gained the world's attention as the city of Beijing prepared to host the 2008 Summer Olympics. Levels of pollution were so high that some people feared that athletes could be in danger. Chinese leaders worked hard to bring air pollution levels down by restricting the numbers of cars on the roads and either closing or moving polluting factories. Air quality did improve slightly in 2008, and China hopes to continue these improvements in the future.

The **Asian Brown Cloud** may affect all nations of Southern and Eastern Asia. It is a brown haze that has many effects on the places it travels above. Some of the effects include the following: it alters monsoon patterns, increases human respiratory problems, and reduces solar radiation to Earth's surface. Toxic waste from factories, motor vehicles, improper cooking fuels, and forest fires all contribute to this cloud of mostly manmade matter.

The Danger of Floods

With so many people living near rivers, the threat of disastrous floods is another major environmental challenge. Over the last 2,000 years, for example, China's Yangtze River has flooded more than 1,000 times. China's Huang He (Yellow River) has caused even more damage. A single massive flood of the Huang He in 1931 killed about four million people. This is considered the deadliest natural disaster in history. This river is sometimes referred to as "China's Sorrow."

Since 1949, the Chinese government has carried out large flood control and irrigation projects to combat the widespread and disastrous flooding. Dams along China's major rivers have helped control the flow and lessen the damage of flooding.

Floods are also a problem in India, where thousands die each year when rivers overflow during monsoon season. When the Brahmaputra River flooded in 2009, about 500,000 people were left homeless. The low-lying country of Bangladesh is vulnerable to flooding as well. Nearly every year, floods destroy crops and kill many people. The main danger from floods comes when floodwaters become polluted. People lose access to clean drinking water, and disease spreads quickly in the polluted water.

Deforestation

Deforestation, or the loss of forests, is a concern in many Asian countries. When rural population increases, deforestation worsens. The reason is that people use the trees for fuel. The Indian government is trying to get people to use biogas instead. **Biogas** is cooking fuel produced by breaking down organic matter. In 1985, a new ministry was created in India called the Ministry of Environment and Forests.

The effects of deforestation

Show What You Know

If you were in charge of an environmental organization within an Asian nation, how would you try to solve your nation's environmental problems? Think about what the specific problems are, who you would get involved to help solve these problems, and what you would do.

_____

_____

_____

_____

_____

_____

_____

_____

_____

_____

_____

_____

_____

_____

_____

_____

_____

_____

_____

_____

_____

_____

Lesson Practice

Circle the letter of the best answer for each item.

Thinking It Through

1. Why did China restrict the use of cars and close factories in Beijing in 2008?

    A. to help clean up the waters of the Yangtze River

    B. to improve air quality before the Olympics

    C. to prevent flooding in rural areas of China

    D. to try to slow economic growth

    Air pollution is a serious problem in many Chinese cities. The government tried to project a positive image of China to the outside world.

2. The many small industrial workshops in India

    A. make it easy for the Indian government to enforce its environmental policies.

    B. make it difficult for the Indian government to enforce its environmental policies.

    C. are the major cause of India's environmental problems.

    D. are run by the government.

    HINT *Environmental policies require that the government enforce them.*

3. What does an examination of environmental policies in Southern and Eastern Asian countries show?

    A. Industrialization has not had an effect on environmental problems.

    B. Only the citizens are able to set environmental policy.

    C. The governments have done little to solve problems.

    D. The governments of Asian countries are working to solve problems.

4. What is "biogas"?

    A. a type of cooking fuel

    B. a food eaten in Southern Asian countries

    C. a type of gas used in vehicles

    D. an air purifier

33 Cultural Features of Southern and Eastern Asia

 SS7G12.a–c

Southern and Eastern Asian countries have a rich cultural range due to their long history and wide variety of ethnic groups. An ethnic group is a cultural community of people with common ancestry, often sharing common religion, language, and traditions.

People from different ethnic groups can belong to the same religious group. Millions of followers of Islam, for instance, live in Indonesia, Pakistan, and other countries throughout Asia. Asia's population includes a diverse variety of religious groups.

Hinduism

Within India, the major religion practiced is **Hinduism**. Hinduism arose from the Aryan Vedic civilization around 1500 BCE. Vedism was the religion of the peoples of the Indus civilization of India. Hindu practices affect many parts of Indian life including literature, arts, and economics. Hinduism is very old and includes a variety of beliefs. It has absorbed ideas from other religions. It is a polytheistic religion, meaning there is belief in many gods.

The main texts of Hinduism are the *Vedas* and *Upanishads*. Hinduism includes a **caste**, or class system of four main classes. The highest caste is the **Brahmans**, or priestly class. In Hinduism, the individual and the universe are part of each other. Hindus also believe in **samsara**, which is life's cycle of death and rebirth. Hindus worship many gods and goddesses. They each have special qualities and symbols. For example, Saraswati is the goddess of music, books, and learning. Music and dance are considered a form of worship and are part of religious celebrations, as well as part of daily life. Hindus celebrate many holidays throughout the year.

The Hindu god Vishnu

Buddhism

Buddhism first spread throughout Asia, but today it is practiced throughout the world. It started in India, like Hinduism. Siddhartha Gautama, a Hindu, was born in Nepal around 563 BCE to a wealthy family. He had never seen sickness or poverty. At age 29, he left home and saw death and sickness for the first time. He wanted to find a place with no suffering. After many years of self-denial and self-torture, he turned to meditation to find an answer.

He was called Buddha, which means the awakened, or "enlightened one." Buddha said people could be free of suffering if they gave up their desires for power and money. Buddha taught the Four Noble Truths. They are: (1) Life has suffering; (2) We suffer because we want power and riches; (3) To not suffer, we need to not want power and riches; and (4) To give up wanting power and riches, we must follow the Eight-Fold Path. The aspects of the Eight-Fold Path are: right understanding, right thought, right speech, right action, right livelihood, right effort, right mindfulness, and right concentration. Like Hindus, Buddhists believe in rebirth and strive to reach nirvana. **Nirvana** is the freeing of the self from material desires. Buddhists often meditate as a way to clear their minds and to experience a glimpse of nirvana.

Buddhist practices differ among countries and sects. Some Buddhists chant instead of meditate. They all believe in respecting others and praying for world peace. Buddhist priests conduct most funerals in Japan today. Many Japanese go to family graves and Buddhist temples to pay respect to ancestors.

Islam

Most of the people in Indonesia, Pakistan, Bangladesh, and Malaysia practice Islam. Many people in India, China, and the Philippines practice it as well. The religion of Islam started in Southwest Asia during the 7th century. People who practice Islam are called Muslims.

Muhammad was born in Mecca, located in present-day Saudi Arabia. On his travels, he saw people worshipping many gods and thought that people were not living the right way. Muhammad said that *Allah* (God) had sent an angel to him. The angel told Muhammad to be Allah's messenger and to tell the Arabs to give up all their gods. Muhammad told the Arabs that there is only one true God, and many people listened to Muhammad and followed his ideas. He destroyed the belief in the many gods that Arabs had worshipped. He brought Arabs together to follow the religion of Islam. Islam then began to spread to other parts of the world.

Muslims believe the Qur'an contains the word of Allah. The Qur'an is the sacred book for Muslims. It states how people should live their lives. All Muslims learn the Five Pillars of Islam, which are faith, prayer, charity, fasting, and pilgrimage, or hajj. The **hajj** is a journey a Muslim makes to Mecca, the holiest city, at least once in a lifetime. Muslims worship in mosques.

Shinto

Shinto is Japan's native religion. Shinto means "the way of the gods." It has neither sacred writings nor an organized set of beliefs or even a founder. It is a religious tradition that stresses the presence of **kami**, or spirits, in everything from plants and animals to rocks and mountains. These spirits control all of the forces of nature. Shinto followers believe that all people after death become kami and continue to participate in their community. In this way, Shinto creates a link between people and the powerful forces of nature.

Followers of Shinto devote time every day to service to the kami. Participation in Shinto traditions and rituals at shrines and in the home are important. When entering a shrine, a Shinto follower passes through a torii, or gate. This symbolizes movement from the finite human world into the infinite world of the gods.

Shinto focuses on giving thanks to the kami. Shinto followers show their appreciation to their ancestors, too. Followers believe that life and all its blessings come from ancestors, so they must be remembered and acknowledged.

Taoism

Taoism is practiced in China. *Tao* in Chinese means "the way." The way represents the flow of life. People are encouraged to live harmoniously by going with the flow, rather than going against it. It is more of a philosophy than a religion. Its founder was Lao Tzu (sometimes spelled Laozi), who wrote the *Tao Te Ching*. This book states Lao Tzu's philosophy. Lao Tzu's book includes statements such as: "Therefore the sage (wise person) manages affairs without doing anything, and conveys his instructions without the use of speech." The Tao forces people to think: "The soft overcomes the hard; and the weak the strong." It includes many observations: "Man at his birth is supple and weak; at his death, firm and strong. (So it is with) all things. Trees and plants, in their early growth, are soft and brittle; at their death, dry and withered." One of the basic principles of Taoism is that opposites work in harmony with one another to balance the whole.

Confucianism

Confucianism is not an organized religion. Rather, it is a philosophy and way of life based on the life and teachings of Confucius. Many people in Eastern Asia follow Buddhism, Taoism, or another religion and still consider themselves to be followers of Confucius.

Confucius

Confucius was a teacher and philosopher who lived in China from 551 BCE to 479 BCE. He taught that life should be dedicated to a constant effort at learning and self-improvement. For Confucius, keys to this effort included education, self-discipline, public service, and a strong commitment to family and tradition. He was a promoter of education, believing that teachers had a vital role to play in improving society. Leaders, Confucius said, should influence others through the example of their moral behavior, rather than the use of force. Followers of Confucius strive to be *junzi*, or exemplary persons, who serve as examples of proper behavior. The ideas and teachings of Confucius continue to influence life in China and other countries of Eastern Asia, including Taiwan, Vietnam, and Korea.

The Arts of Southern and Eastern Asia

India's most cherished literature includes the Sanskrit epics, the *Mahabharata* and the *Ramayana*, both written long before the Common Era. Poet Rabindranath Tagore won the Nobel Prize for literature in 1913.

Throughout the centuries, Indian architecture has reflected several different influences. Stupas, or sacred burial mounds, came out of Buddhist architectural traditions. Muslim invaders changed Indian architecture to include domes, mosaics, and minarets. A minaret is the part of a mosque that is a tall tower from which Muslims are called to worship. The Taj Mahal, in northern India, is world famous for its architecture, which is a blend of Indian, Persian, and Islamic styles.

Indonesia offers various forms of art and culture because of the many different ethnicities there. The architecture there has had many influences and often includes leaf decorations. Indonesians have their own pop and rock music stars, although there are many people who continue to listen to traditional music. There are also traditional dances, like the Javanese and Balinese. Furthermore, Indonesians have their own cuisine, which is typically simpler than other Southern and Eastern Asian dishes.

The Arts of Eastern Asia

China has the longest literary history of any nation in the world. Drama has a place in China's history, as does the novel. Early Chinese novels include *The Romance of the Three Kingdoms* and *The Journey to the West*. **Calligraphy**, or brush painting of Chinese characters on silk or paper, is a highly respected art form in China. Painting, sculpture, and architecture are also important in Chinese society. Music has a rich tradition in Chinese society. One example of a Chinese musical instrument is a **qin**. This is a long, seven-stringed zither that is plucked with the fingers.

Peking Opera, as it is called in the West, is called **jingxi** in Chinese, meaning "drama of the capital city." Jingxi started in the late 18th century and it uses a variety of art forms including music, acrobatics, speech, and martial arts to tell a story. In it, male actors play both male and female roles.

Japan is well-known for its dramatic theater, which started around the 7th century. Theater often blended drama, music, and dance. In the 16th century, the puppet theater became popular. During the 17th century, **Kabuki theater** surpassed the puppet theater in popularity. Kabuki is often about historical events or love relationships. Actors use an old-fashioned form of the Japanese language and traditional Japanese instruments accompany their words. Audience members will often shout a favorite Kabuki actor's name during a performance. **Haiku** is a form of unrhymed poetry of three lines and a specific number of syllables per line that developed in Japan and continues to flourish there and throughout the world.

Literacy Rates and Development

India's literacy rate is approximately 65%; Indonesia's literacy rate is 85%; China's literacy rate is 91%; and Japan's literacy rate is 99%. The countries listed here with the highest literacy rates—Japan and China—are more developed than the countries with the lower literacy rates—India and Indonesia, although India's literacy rate is growing quickly. Places with higher literacy rates advance more quickly in the fields of science and technology. This helps a nation become more successful. Countries with higher literacy rates also have lower rates of unemployment.

Show What You Know

Fill in the chart below to show the major religions and arts practiced in the countries listed. One box has already been filled in.

	Major religion	Arts and Literature
India	Hinduism	
Indonesia		
China		
Japan		

Lesson Practice

Thinking It Through

1. According to Confucius, how should leaders influence others?

   A. by use of force

   B. by following the Eight-Fold Path

   C. by the example of their moral behavior

   D. by studying philosophy

Confucianism is a philosophy and a way of life. Followers of Confucius strive to be exemplary persons.

2. Hinduism and Buddhism both seek

   A. nirvana.

   B. haiku.

   C. kabuki.

   D. qin.

   HINT *They both seek to free themselves from worldly attachments.*

3. Which religion requires a hajj?

   A. Hinduism

   B. Shinto

   C. Islam

   D. Buddhism

4. The *Mahabharata* and the *Ramayana* are Sanskrit epics of

   A. China.

   B. India.

   C. Japan.

   D. Indonesia.

34 Southern and Eastern Asian Governments

 SS7CG7.a

The Republic of India

India is the world's largest democracy. The country is a federal republic, meaning power is shared between the national government and state governments. India is also a parliamentary democracy.

India's government has three main branches. The executive branch consists of the president, who is the chief of state; the prime minister, who is the head of the government; and the Council of Ministers, who make up the cabinet. The legislative branch is a **bicameral** parliament, meaning it has two law-making groups: the Rajya Sabha, or Council of States, and the Lok Sabha, or House of the People. The judicial branch is made up of the Supreme Court, which has a chief justice along with 25 other judges. The prime minister advises the president regarding which judges to appoint.

The president's duties are mostly ceremonial. The prime minister, who is the real head of state, is chosen by the vote in the House of the People. The Council of Ministers must also answer to the House of the People.

India has many political parties. The biggest ones are the Bharatiya Janata Party, the Indian National Congress, and the Janata Dal (United Party). Indians 18 years of age and older can vote. The basic rights of citizens are protected by the constitution, which is a list of "fundamental rights" of all citizens.

China's Communist State

China's Communist Party leads the nation. Under China's constitution, the highest organ of state power is the National People's Congress (NPC). China has three branches of government. The executive branch includes a president (head of state), vice president, State Council, and premier (head of government). The legislative branch is **unicameral**, consisting only of the National People's Congress (NPC). The judicial branch includes the Supreme People's Court.

Chinese Communists

The NPC meets for two weeks every year. The State Council presents new policies, laws, budgets, and personnel changes to the NPC. The NPC can debate anything that is presented to them. These meetings are not open to the public. The NPC can make changes to what the State Council has recommended. The Standing Committee carries out state power when the NPC is not meeting for its two-week session.

The largest political party is the Chinese Communist Party (CCP) with as many as 70 million members. Eight minor political parties operate under Communist supervision. The CCP is highly authoritarian, meaning it completely controls the Chinese government. The CCP sets policies that the government must enforce.

However, the CCP has some checks on its control. China is a large country with a massive population. This poses problems for the CCP. The population is also diverse with many ethnic minorities. The CCP must work throughout all levels of society, including in the government, in the economy, and in cultural institutions to make sure that non-Communist organizations do not challenge Communist rule. Communist rule is strongest in urban areas, but most of the people live in rural areas, where Communist control is less dominant.

Men and women 18 years of age and older can vote in elections to choose local representatives to the People's Congress. Citizens, however, have very little power when it comes to selecting national leaders or influencing national policies. The Chinese constitution calls for the protection of human rights, but these rights are often not protected. The government restricts citizens' freedom of speech, press, and religion, and routinely jails people for expressing political views in opposition to those of the Communist leaders.

Throughout history, the Chinese people have united to overthrow corrupt governments. Starting in the spring of 1989, college students, intellectuals, and others in China's major cities started demonstrating in the state capital for more freedom to be guaranteed in their constitution. They also called for an end to government corruption.

Japan's Constitutional Monarchy

Japan has a constitutional monarchy with a parliamentary form of government. The government has three branches. The executive branch includes a cabinet made up of the prime minister (head of government) and ministers of state, who are all civilians. A **civilian** is a person who is not part of the military of a country. Ministers are appointed or removed by the prime minister. The prime minister is chosen by his colleagues in the **Diet**, the country's parliament. The Diet includes the House of Representatives and House of Councilors. The judicial branch is a civil law system based on the model of Roman law. It is independent from the other two branches. The Supreme Court is the highest judicial authority.

In Japan, people can vote at age 20 and above. Secret ballots are used to elect people to office. People's fundamental human rights are specifically protected in the constitution. While the Japanese people are in control of their nation's sovereignty, Japan still has an emperor, who is the symbol of the state. He is basically a figurehead without much official power. Japan has 47 prefectures, or governed districts. Political leaders of prefectures are elected by popular vote for four-year terms. Most prefectures get support from Japan's central government. They are not sovereign states in the way that states are in the United States.

Show What You Know

Fill in the chart below to review the governments of India, China, and Japan. The first box has been filled in for you.

	India	China	Japan
Type of Government	federal republic		
Main Leader(s)			
Branches of Government			
Voting Age			

Lesson Practice

Circle the letter of the best answer for each item.

Thinking It Through

1. Which of the following is true about India's form of government?

   A. States have little power in government.

   B. People can vote at age 14.

   C. A prime minister is the head of government.

   D. There are two branches of government.

   Many components of India's government are similar to other republics throughout the world. In parliamentary democracies, the president has mainly symbolic powers over government.

2. Which of the following countries is MOSTLY controlled by one political party?

   A. India

   B. Indonesia

   C. China

   D. Japan

   HINT *In this country, the main political party controls all parts of society, including the government, the economy, and cultural institutions.*

3. Of the following choices, the country that still has an emperor is

   A. India.

   B. Indonesia.

   C. China.

   D. Japan.

4. What is common to BOTH India and China and affects how these governments must deal with their people?

   A. Their Communist parties have control of the countryside.

   B. Most of their populations live in villages or rural areas.

   C. Their emperors are still highly respected by the people.

   D. The executive branches of each government are made up of commoners.

35 Southern and Eastern Asian Trade

 SS7E9.a–c

International trade is a huge part of the economies of Southern and Eastern Asia. In fact, China is now the second-largest exporter in the world, behind only Germany. China exports goods worth nearly $1.5 trillion dollars each year. Japan is the world's fourth-largest exporter, with annual exports worth about $750 billion. China and Japan are examples of countries that benefit greatly from international trade. Massive export earnings fuel economic growth and help create new jobs.

Japan and International Trade

Japan lacks many natural resources and must import huge amounts of food, fuel, and raw materials. Japan compensates for this by specializing in the production of manufactured goods, such as cars and electronics. Earnings from these exports allow Japan to buy the goods it needs from overseas.

For the majority of the years from 1965 on, Japan experienced a trade surplus, meaning it exported more than it imported. This also means that the country brings in more money than it pays out. Japanese companies used these trade surpluses to invest in foreign stocks, bonds, real estate, and business ventures. This has many benefits for the Japanese companies. Land and labor are often cheaper in foreign countries than they are in Japan. Interestingly, today Japanese companies produce more cars and consumer electronics outside of Japan than within Japan.

Pacific Rim Countries

The countries that border the Pacific Ocean are referred to as the **Pacific Rim**. Economically, the Pacific Rim has become very powerful. Now the value of goods crossing over the Pacific Ocean is greater than the value of goods crossing over the Atlantic Ocean. A huge portion of this trade moves from China to the United States. China's exports to the U.S. are worth more than $300 billion a year.

Migration of people within the Pacific Rim is also becoming more common. Transnationalism is occurring in the Pacific Rim, too. **Transnationalism** is when people legally live and work in more than one country. Tourism also helps to connect these nations.

Some nations recognize that transnationalism can directly help their countries. South Korea, for example, encourages its entrepreneurs to go to California. The South Korean government has created the Overseas Korea Foundation. This organization helps Koreans abroad. The government knows that when their citizens are abroad, they will purchase Korean-made goods in the nations where they are living.

Southern and Eastern Asia's Economic Power

Four places in Asia used to be known as the "Four Asian Tigers": South Korea, Taiwan, Singapore, and Hong Kong. Taiwan, according to mainland China, is a part of China and not a separate nation. Taiwan claims to be an independent nation. Taiwan continues to be an economic powerhouse. Singapore is an independent nation. In 1997, Hong Kong once again became a part of mainland China. For almost one hundred years, Hong Kong had been a part of Great Britain. The economies of these four places remain strong.

Trade Barriers and How They Are Overcome

Governments sometimes use trade barriers to limit what can be traded to their people and with whom their people can trade. A country can impose a tariff, or a tax on imports, to help a certain industry. Tariffs damage a country's international trade, however, by making foreign goods more expensive.

Aerial view of Hong Kong

In India, for example, the government has a large amount of control over foreign trade and investment. India traditionally had high tariffs. Nonagricultural items that are imported had a 20% tariff. This discouraged Indians from buying nonagricultural items made in other countries. By 2006, however, India had lowered its tariffs to 12.5%. These changes helped to increase foreign trade and investment in India.

Import quotas are another form of trade barrier. Quotas limit the number of goods that can be imported from a certain country. It has a similar effect to tariffs, because it makes a certain item harder to get, and thus, more expensive.

An embargo, or ban on trade with a certain country, is normally put in place for political reasons. In 2009, for instance, the United Nations voted to impose trade embargoes on North Korea. This was done to punish North Korea for testing nuclear bombs and long-range missiles, in violation of a UN order.

A shaky or poor economy can act as another kind of trade barrier. Indonesia struggles with many economic problems. Foreign countries will view investment in the nation as too high a risk. However, Indonesia has taken steps to show that its economy can overcome problems. It suffered greatly in the Asian financial crisis of the late 1990s. As a result, it had to take a huge loan from the International Monetary Fund (IMF). Indonesia was able to pay back its IMF debt in October of 2006. This was four years ahead of schedule. Actions like this help to build the confidence of international investors.

Currency Exchange

To engage in international trade, nations need a system to exchange currency. An exchange rate is set so that countries can purchase and sell items in different countries. Exchange rates vary daily.

The rupee is the basic currency of India. As of the end of 2009, roughly 45 rupees equaled one U.S. dollar. The basic unit of currency in China is the yuan. Roughly 7 yuan equaled one U.S. dollar. The yen is the basic unit of currency in Japan. Approximately 92 yen equaled one U.S. dollar.

Show What You Know

Discuss reasons why a Pacific Rim nation would be a good place to live. Write your answer in the space provided.

Lesson Practice

DIRECTIONS
Circle the letter of the best answer for each item.

Thinking It Through

1. The Indonesian government has taken steps to make the country stronger economically. What results MOST LIKELY will follow?

    The Indonesian government has tried to make changes that will benefit Indonesia. They know that other people must regain confidence in Indonesia.

    A. Other governments will question the government's drastic steps.

    B. Foreign investors may want to invest in Indonesia.

    C. Communist economic policies will once again take hold.

    D. They will never experience another natural disaster.

2. A trend that is meeting with success in the Pacific Rim is

    A. communism.

    B. underdevelopment.

    C. transnationalism.

    D. trade deficits.

    HINT *This occurs when people legally live and work in more than one country.*

3. Japan has a trade surplus. This means that it

    A. exports more than it imports.

    B. imports more than it exports.

    C. has extra unsold goods for sale.

    D. transfers extra goods to Japanese companies abroad.

4. All of the following are trade barriers EXCEPT

    A. quotas.

    B. tariffs.

    C. foreign investment.

    D. embargoes.

36 Southern and Eastern Asian Economies

 SS7E8.c, SS7E10.a–d

Comparing Economic Systems

The countries of Southern and Eastern Asia use a variety of economic systems. While most have mixed economies, the role of governments varies from place to place. India, for example, has a mixed economy in which the government makes some economic decisions, and businesses and individuals make other decisions. Until recently, much of India's economy was planned by the central government. Since the 1990s, however, government reforms have allowed more economic freedom and decreased some regulations. This has helped fuel fast growth in India in the past decade.

For many years after the rise of communism in China, the country had a command economy. The state owned most of the country's factories and industries. Since Mao Zedong's death in 1976, his successors have focused on market-oriented economic reforms. In these years, the Chinese standard of living has improved, and output for China's economy has quadrupled. The private sector has grown rapidly, with more privately-owned companies. An increasing amount of economic activity takes place outside government control. While China has a mixed economy today, the government still controls parts of the economy. For example, government officials set prices for energy and other key goods, and set wage levels.

Japan has a mixed economy in which the government plays an active and important role. The specific role of Japan's government in the economy is unique to Japan. While the government does not have official control over the economy, government leaders consult with business leaders. Together they agree on long-term plans, targets for production, and how to use the nation's resources. When the economy of Japan began to slow in the 1990s, many blamed the government's active role in the economy. In the years since, Japan has worked toward the goal of reducing government involvement. The hope is that free market forces can help energize growth and create new jobs.

Unlike the countries described above, North Korea has a true command economy. The national government controls all aspects of the economy, deciding what gets produced, how it gets made, and how much it should cost. This system has proved unsuccessful in meeting the nation's goals, leaving the economy too weak to provide for its people. When floods and droughts hit North Korea in the 1990s, the country was unable to cope, and there was mass starvation. Since then, North Korea has begun allowing small amounts of foreign investment, though the economy remains solidly in government hands. The country continues to rely on foreign aid, and living standards today are lower than they were 20 years ago.

Factors Influencing Economic Growth

Measured in gross domestic product (GDP), China, Japan, and India are all among the world's largest economies. In fact, these countries run second, third, and fourth in the world respectively—only the U.S. economy is larger. As of 2009, China's GDP stood at nearly $8 trillion. Japan's was just over $4 trillion, and India's was over $3 trillion. In all three countries, strong investments in capital resources such as factories and technologies are important contributors to economic growth.

Education and training are also major factors. In India, 59.5% of the population age 15 and over can read and write. But this low figure masks an important fact: a significant portion of India's population is well educated and speaks English. This group of workers is a very valuable asset to India. The country's labor force is thriving because of **outsourcing**. Many companies in the United States outsource their work. This means that they hire people in other countries and pay them lower wages to do certain types of work. American computer companies, for instance, hire people in India to give technical support to their customers. In addition to outsourcing, India is a major exporter of software services and software workers.

The government is also improving the basic infrastructure of Indian society, which will help the rural poor. Infrastructure includes systems such as communications, transportation, power lines, and buildings such as schools. India's natural resources are important to the economy as well. It has the fourth-largest coal reserves in the world. India has natural gas, petroleum, diamonds, limestone, land suitable for farming, and a variety of metal deposits. Yet water pollution and nondrinkable tap water in many places are major problems in India.

In recent decades, the Chinese made a strong commitment to educating and training its population. This investment in human capital has paid off. The national literacy rate is now over 90%. This has helped create a large pool of well-trained workers, which helps fuel the rapid growth of China's factories and high-tech industries. China also has a large group of entrepreneurs who are willing to take great risks to try to achieve financial success.

China's economic growth is also helped by its many natural resources, including the world's largest potential for hydropower, as well as coal, petroleum, and natural gas. The Chinese government has invested heavily in the Three Gorges Dam, across the Yangtze River. The project cost $24 billion and took thirteen years to complete. It will vastly improve electrification and flood control in the Yangtze basin.

Unlike India and China, Japan lacks abundant natural resources and must import raw materials and energy. With only a small amount of fertile soil, a very small portion of the population works on farms. Also unlike India and China, Japan has lower levels of entrepreneurship. It is difficult for small businesses to get loans and to move quickly to produce new goods or services. Many in Japan believe this has been a factor in the economy's poor performance in recent years. Government officials are committed to encouraging entrepreneurs in years ahead.

Japan has made up for what it lacks by investing heavily in education and industry. Japan's literacy rate of over 99% reflects the country's commitment to education. Japan's well-trained workforce has been a major key to the country's success since World War II.

Japan's schools are very competitive and challenging.

Show What You Know

Using your basic knowledge of economics, explain why so many Southern and Eastern Asian nations use a mixed economy. Write your answer in the space provided.

_____

_____

_____

_____

_____

_____

_____

_____

_____

_____

_____

Lesson Practice

Thinking It Through

1. Which of the following countries does NOT have one of the world's highest GDPs?

   A. India

   B. China

   C. North Korea

   D. Japan

   > *India, China, and Japan have various forms of mixed economies. North Korea has a command economy. Government-planned economies usually do not grow rapidly.*

2. How does a high literacy rate usually affect a nation's economy?

   A. Countries with high literacy rates often have good economies.

   B. Literacy rates have little effect on nations' economies.

   C. A high literacy rate equals a poor economy.

   D. People who can read do not contribute to the economy.

   HINT *Literacy rate is the percent of people who can read and write in a nation.*

3. The economic system that is practiced MOST in Southern and Eastern Asian countries is a

   A. market economy.

   B. traditional economy.

   C. command economy.

   D. mixed economy.

4. Many American companies hire Indian companies to do work that used to be done in the U.S. This is an example of

   A. tariffs.

   B. outsourcing.

   C. communism.

   D. manufacturing.

4 Review

Choose the best answer for each question. Fill in the circle in the spaces provided on your answer sheet.

1. Beginning with President Eisenhower, several U.S. presidents expanded U.S. military involvement in Vietnam. The main goal of the U.S. effort was to

   A. assist the Viet Cong to rebuild North Vietnam.

   B. stop China from making Vietnam a colony.

   C. stop Communist forces from taking over the whole nation.

   D. support the presidency of Ho Chi Minh.

2. All of the following are causes of pollution in the Ganges River EXCEPT

   A. exhaust from cars in Calcutta.

   B. human waste flowing into the river.

   C. pollution from factories entering the water.

   D. fertilizers from farms flowing into the river.

3. Which statement illustrates a major difference between North Korea and South Korea?

   A. South Korea is a Communist country, and North Korea is a democratic country.

   B. North Korea is a Communist country, and South Korea is a democratic country.

   C. The Soviet Union still controls North Korea as a colony.

   D. The United States still controls North Korea as a colony.

4. Which of the following countries built the Three Gorges Dam across the Yangtze River?

   A. Pakistan

   B. China

   C. India

   D. Indonesia

5. Which of the following statements is true?

   A. Buddhism is older than Hinduism.

   B. Buddhism developed out of Hinduism.

   C. Islam has its beginnings in Hinduism.

   D. Islam is older than Hinduism.

6. Japan's commitment to excellent, highly competitive schools is an example of the country's investment in

   A. human capital.

   B. capital goods.

   C. natural resources.

   D. entrepreneurial class.

7. The governments of India, China, and Japan all

   A. have the Communist party as the dominant political party.

   B. have an emperor or king as a figurehead.

   C. contain only a judicial branch of government.

   D. contain three main branches of government.

8. In general, countries like Japan and China with higher literacy rates

   A. have children start attending schools at age 7.

   B. have higher standards of living than nations with lower literacy rates.

   C. also have much more competitive elementary schools.

   D. focus on mathematics less than on reading and writing.

9. Unlike the nations of Japan and South Korea, China has had to deal with which of the following problems?

   A. flooding of the Huang He (Yellow River)

   B. pollution from industry

   C. overfishing of its waters

   D. environmental activists

10. Which country did Vietnam gain independence from in 1954?

   A. Britain

   B. China

   C. France

   D. Japan

11. Which nation would not be considered a part of the Pacific Rim, since it does not border the Pacific Ocean?

   A. China

   B. India

   C. Japan

   D. Philippines

12. Shinto is the major religion practiced in

   A. Indonesia.

   B. China.

   C. Japan.

   D. India.

13. One of the deadliest natural disasters of all time was caused by

    A. flooding of the Huang He (Yellow River).
    B. water pollution in the Yangtze River.
    C. air pollution in Indian cities.
    D. an earthquake in Pakistan's capital.

14. Which of the following nations is an archipelago?

    A. Japan
    B. Bangladesh
    C. India
    D. North Korea

15. Mohandas Gandhi is BEST remembered as

    A. the head of the Communist revolution in Vietnam.
    B. the leader of India's movement to achieve independence from Britain.
    C. president of the East India Company in the 1800s.
    D. China's most famous nationalist leader.

16. People from different ethnic groups can belong to the same religious group. Which religion has followers in Indonesia, Pakistan, and other Southern and Eastern Asian countries?

    A. Shinto
    B. Islam
    C. Confucianism
    D. Hinduism

Use the map below to answer question 17.

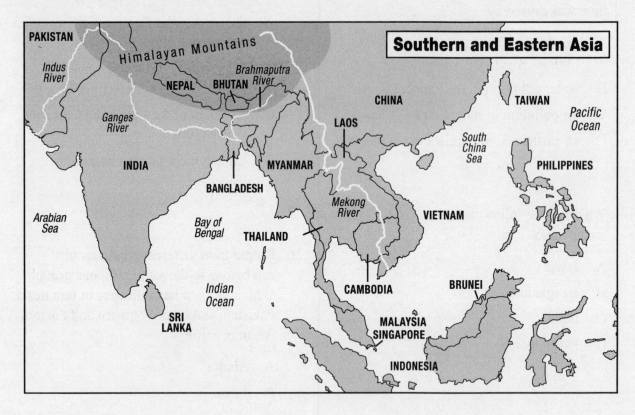

17. The Himalayan Mountains cover parts of all the following countries EXCEPT

   A. China.

   B. India.

   C. Nepal.

   D. Bangladesh.

18. Which river flows through Laos, Cambodia, and Vietnam?

   A. Ganges

   B. Brahmaputra

   C. Mekong

   D. Indus

19. To improve air quality in Beijing, the Chinese government

    A. created new national parks.

    B. built the Three Gorges Dam.

    C. encouraged the use of biogas.

    D. restricted the use of cars.

20. Which is the basic unit of currency used in China?

    A. pound

    B. rupee

    C. yuan

    D. yen

21. After World War II, Korea was

    A. controlled in the north by the Soviet Union.

    B. controlled in the south by the Soviet Union.

    C. completely controlled by the Soviet Union.

    D. controlled in the north by the United States.

22. Which of the following countries must import MOST of the natural resources and fuel it needs?

    A. India

    B. Japan

    C. China

    D. Vietnam

23. One of the MAIN reasons the United States occupied Japan after World War II was that

   A. China wanted this to happen since Japan had taken over China prior to World War II.

   B. Japan already showed that it was incapable of governing itself as shown by the puppet government of Manchukuo.

   C. the United States never wanted Japan to be a militaristic power again.

   D. Japan's economy was already strong; it just needed help with its government.

24. Of the following choices, which type of climate allows for larger population densities?

   A. arctic

   B. sub-arctic

   C. arid

   D. temperate

25. Which of the following nations had a command economy for many years, but has since changed to a mixed economy?

   A. North Korea

   B. China

   C. Japan

   D. South Korea

26. One environmental problem that can affect India, Indonesia, and Pakistan is

   A. the Asia Brown Cloud.

   B. pollution of the Ganges River.

   C. overflowing of the Huang He (Yellow River).

   D. flooding in Bangladesh.

27. When North Korea tested nuclear weapons in 2009, the United Nations responded by

   A. imposing a tariff.

   B. imposing an embargo.

   C. imposing a quota.

   D. imposing an arms agreement.

28. The Gobi Desert is located in

    A. India.

    B. Japan.

    C. Pakistan.

    D. China.

29. In the last 20 years, what action has India taken in order to increase trade with other nations?

    A. adopt a new currency

    B. lower tariffs

    C. raise tariffs

    D. impose quotas

30. Why do many Japanese companies invest in overseas companies?

    A. Land and labor is often cheaper than in Japan.

    B. They are trying to take over countries the way they did during World War II.

    C. The Japanese emperor gives companies money to invest overseas.

    D. More cars are being produced within Japan than in the rest of the world.

31. Mao Zedong's program to renew the spirit of the Chinese revolution was called the

    A. Great Leap Forward.

    B. Cultural Revolution.

    C. Bourgeois Revolution.

    D. Long March.

32. China has many of these people. They are willing to take big risks with hopes of achieving financial success. What are they called?

    A. communists

    B. entrepreneurs

    C. bourgeoisie

    D. guerrillas

33. The economy of North Korea is described as a

   A. market economy.

   B. mixed economy.

   C. command economy.

   D. traditional economy.

34. As a result of huge investments in industry, which country now has the world's second highest GDP?

   A. China

   B. South Korea

   C. India

   D. Vietnam

35. Which type of environment in Southern and Eastern Asia is MOST densely populated?

   A. mountains

   B. deserts

   C. river plains

   D. wetlands

36. India's form of government is described as

   A. a constitutional monarchy.

   B. a unitary republic.

   C. a parliamentary democracy.

   D. an authoritarian regime.

Georgia CRCT Coach, GPS Edition, Social Studies, Grade 7

POSTTEST

Name: _____

General Instructions

Today you will be taking a test similar to the Social Studies Criterion-Referenced Competency Test. The Social Studies test consists of multiple-choice questions. A sample has been included. The sample shows you how to mark your answers. There are several important things to remember.

- Answer all questions on your answer sheet. Do not mark any answers to questions in your test booklet.

- For each question, choose the best answer, and completely fill in the circle in the space provided on your answer sheet.

- If you do not know the answer to a question, skip it and go on. You may return to it later if you have time.

- If you finish the section of the test that you are working on early, you may review your answers in that section only. You may not review another section or go on to the next section of the test.

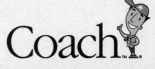

Sample Question

The sample test question below is provided to show you what the questions in the test are like and how to mark your answer to each question. For each question, choose the one best answer, and fill in the circle in the space provided on your answer sheet for the answer you have chosen. Be sure to mark all of your answers to the questions on your answer sheet.

Sample

1. Which of the following countries was NOT considered one of the Asian Tigers?

   A. South Korea

   B. North Korea

   C. Singapore

   D. Taiwan

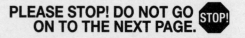

PLEASE STOP! DO NOT GO ON TO THE NEXT PAGE.

Section 1

Section 1 of this test has thirty questions. Choose the best answer for each question. Fill in the circle in the spaces provided for questions 1 through 30 on your answer sheet.

1. In which country would you find the mouth of the Brahmaputra River and the Ganges River, the shadow of the Himalayan Mountains, and the country's border on the Bay of Bengal?

    A. India

    B. Bangladesh

    C. Pakistan

    D. Sri Lanka

2. A geologist in search of rock formations that might indicate petroleum reserves would MOST LIKELY find them in

    A. Nigeria.

    B. South Africa.

    C. Mali.

    D. Kenya.

3. Which reason explains how Japan was able to rebound from defeat in World War II and become an economic power?

    A. abundant natural resources for manufacturing

    B. economic assistance from the Soviet Union

    C. rebuilding assistance from the United States

    D. growing military industrial complex

4. The majority of the people of India follow which religion?

    A. Islam

    B. Taoism

    C. Buddhism

    D. Hinduism

PLEASE GO ON TO THE NEXT PAGE.

POSTTEST

5. The government in Saudi Arabia is a

   A. democracy.

   B. republic.

   C. confederacy.

   D. monarchy.

6. The religion of Islam is split into sects. The majority of Muslims belong to which sect?

   A. Shi'a

   B. Kurd

   C. Hindi

   D. Sunni

7. Japan is one of the world's leading exporters and also one of the world's largest importers. Which of these products would Japan MOST LIKELY import?

   A. oil

   B. cars

   C. electronics

   D. trucks

8. Which of the following is NOT a trade barrier?

   A. government instability

   B. reduction in tariffs

   C. tightening of foreign investment rules

   D. institution of a command economy

PLEASE GO ON TO THE NEXT PAGE.

POSTTEST

9. The Organization of Petroleum Exporting Countries (OPEC) would be concerned with all of the following activities EXCEPT

    A. regulating oil prices.

    B. limiting oil production.

    C. coordinating political objectives for member nations.

    D. expanding iron ore mining.

10. Through technological advances in irrigation, which country turned the Negev Desert into a leading agricultural region?

    A. Syria

    B. Iraq

    C. Jordan

    D. Israel

11. Which organization voted to create the state of Israel in 1948?

    A. League of Nations

    B. United Nations

    C. European Union

    D. World Jewish Federation

12. After which war did the Ottoman Empire officially come to an end?

    A. Vietnam War

    B. World War II

    C. World War I

    D. U.S. Civil War

PLEASE GO ON TO THE NEXT PAGE.

POSTTEST

13. The Five Pillars represent the main beliefs of which major religion?

   A. Islam

   B. Christianity

   C. Judaism

   D. Buddhism

14. Countries in Africa have undergone a wide range of economic development. Which statement illustrates the relationship between literacy and economic growth?

   A. As the literacy rate rises, economic growth declines.

   B. As economic growth rises, the literacy rate declines.

   C. As the literacy rate increases, economic growth rises.

   D. As economic growth declines, the literacy rate declines.

15. Which statement describes the result of fertile soil along the Niger River?

   A. East Africa is the population center of Africa.

   B. South Africa is the population center of Africa.

   C. North Africa is the population center of Africa.

   D. West Africa is the population center of Africa.

16. The Nile River flows through which of the following countries?

   A. Mali

   B. Ethiopia

   C. Libya

   D. Sudan

PLEASE GO ON TO THE NEXT PAGE.

17. The 1977 Camp David Accords were a peace agreement between which two countries?

A. Israel and Syria

B. Iran and Iraq

C. Saudi Arabia and Iran

D. Israel and Egypt

18. As China becomes an economic superpower, it continues to change from a communist, command economy to a

A. pure market economy.

B. mixed economy.

C. Marxist economy.

D. traditional economy.

19. Which of the following countries has built a successful economy without relying on oil sales?

A. Saudi Arabia

B. Iran

C. Turkey

D. Kuwait

20. Members of the African Union hope to increase trade in Africa. One way they hope to achieve this goal is by

A. increasing tariffs on farm products.

B. removing trade barriers between nations.

C. setting import quotas for member nations.

D. imposing embargoes on each other.

PLEASE GO ON TO THE NEXT PAGE.

POSTTEST

Use the map below to answer questions 21 and 22.

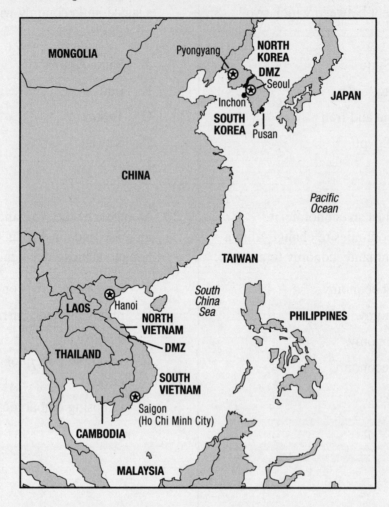

21. In which two countries shown on the map did the United States fight wars during the Cold War?

    A. China and Japan

    B. Korea and Vietnam

    C. Thailand and Philippines

    D. Mongolia and Malaysia

22. The Ho Chi Minh trail connected North Vietnam to South Vietnam through which two neighboring countries?

    A. China and Laos

    B. Laos and Thailand

    C. Laos and Cambodia

    D. Thailand and Cambodia

PLEASE GO ON TO THE NEXT PAGE.

POSTTEST

23. Which country's economy benefits from having educated, English-speaking workers?

    A. India

    B. Jordan

    C. North Korea

    D. Pakistan

24. Islam is the main religion in all of the following countries EXCEPT

    A. Pakistan.

    B. Bangladesh.

    C. India.

    D. Indonesia.

25. Egypt has been called "the gift of the Nile" because of the consistent flooding and the fertile layer of silt deposited along its banks. Which step did the Egyptian government take to maintain better control of those flood waters?

    A. limited access to Luxor

    B. built the Aswan Dam

    C. increased irrigation along the delta

    D. redirected the Nile River

26. Which of the following is NOT an area where you would expect to find a large population in Southwest Asia?

    A. Tigris and Euphrates river valleys

    B. the Jordan River valley

    C. Mediterranean coastline

    D. Saudi Arabia's Rub al Khali Desert

27. What is the governmental system in China today?

    A. communist

    B. republic

    C. democratic

    D. monarchy

PLEASE GO ON TO THE NEXT PAGE.

POSTTEST

28. Although South Africa has had a long association with Great Britain, it does NOT base its currency on the British pound, as many other former colonies do. What is the name of the South African currency?

   A. kroner

   B. dollar

   C. mark

   D. rand

29. Which country would be MOST concerned with the water quality of the Niger River?

   A. Egypt

   B. Mali

   C. Chad

   D. Sudan

30. In which two countries would you find the Gobi Desert?

   A. India and Pakistan

   B. Mongolia and China

   C. China and Russia

   D. Iran and Iraq

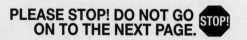

PLEASE STOP! DO NOT GO ON TO THE NEXT PAGE.

Section 2

Section 2 of this test has thirty questions. Choose the best answer for each question. Fill in the circle in the spaces provided for questions 31 through 60 on your answer sheet.

31. Because of an abundance of natural resources, which country has the MOST opportunity for economic development?

    A. Sudan

    B. Egypt

    C. Chad

    D. South Africa

32. Which of these countries does NOT have one of the world's highest gross domestic products?

    A. China

    B. India

    C. Japan

    D. North Korea

Use the list below to answer question 33.
- north of Syria
- west of Iran
- borders Mediterranean Sea

33. Which country is described by the list above?

    A. Iraq

    B. Turkey

    C. Jordan

    D. Kuwait

34. Of the following, which two countries have the highest literacy rates and are more developed as a result?

    A. India and Indonesia

    B. China and India

    C. India and Japan

    D. Japan and China

PLEASE GO ON TO THE NEXT PAGE.

POSTTEST

35. The leader of Israel's government is the prime minister. He or she is a member of the legislature. Israel's form of government is described as a

A. presidential democracy.

B. theocratic republic.

C. parliamentary democracy.

D. constitutional monarchy.

36. Which country has no permanent rivers within its borders and must rely on drilling wells and sparse rainfall for its fresh water?

A. Lebanon

B. Saudi Arabia

C. Iran

D. Turkey

37. Which of the following countries is an archipelago?

A. Indonesia

B. South Korea

C. Vietnam

D. North Korea

38. Which anti-apartheid leader became president of South Africa in 1994?

A. Mansa Musa

B. Nelson Mandela

C. Zara Yakob

D. Frederik Willem de Klerk

39. Which country gained control of land as a result of the Six-Day War in 1967?

A. Israel

B. Syria

C. Saudi Arabia

D. Lebanon

PLEASE GO ON TO THE NEXT PAGE.

POSTTEST

40. Since 1991, India has enjoyed increased foreign trade because of all of the following government steps EXCEPT

A. market-oriented economic reforms.

B. reduction in tariffs.

C. liberalization of foreign investment rules.

D. institution of a command economy.

41. The growing industrial pollution of the Ganges River MOST affects the people of which country?

A. India

B. Indonesia

C. China

D. Pakistan

42. What is the BEST description of the Swahili religion?

A. mixture of Egyptian and Greek beliefs

B. mixture of Islam and traditional beliefs

C. mixture of Bantu and Christian traditions

D. mixture of Judaism and Christianity

43. When a country makes a strong investment in human capital, the MOST LIKELY outcome will be

A. no economic growth.

B. improved economy and gross domestic product.

C. lower gross domestic product.

D. lower literacy rate nationwide.

PLEASE GO ON TO THE NEXT PAGE.

44. One class of people who helps fuel China's growth does so by investing money in the hopes of making a profit. Which term describes this class of people?

   A. brokers

   B. bankers

   C. entrepreneurs

   D. chief executive officers

45. Since the withdrawal of Israeli troops, where in the present-day country of Israel have the Palestinian people begun self-rule in an effort to establish a Palestinian state?

   A. Golan Heights

   B. Negev

   C. Haifa

   D. Gaza Strip

46. The main goal of the Pan-African movement was to

   A. erect new trade barriers with Europe.

   B. encourage all Africans to work together.

   C. promote apartheid in Africa.

   D. gain colonies in overseas territories.

47. Which present-day country did Abraham, the father of the Hebrew people, originally call home?

   A. Iraq

   B. Iran

   C. Israel

   D. Egypt

PLEASE GO ON TO THE NEXT PAGE.

48. Desertification is a major problem in Africa today. Which country has made a huge effort, along with its neighbor, Tanzania, to plant trees along the Serengeti Plain to stop the spread of the desert?

A. South Africa

B. Mali

C. Uganda

D. Kenya

49. In recent years, Saudi Arabia's leaders have worked to diversify the economy by investing in capital resources. Which of the following is NOT a capital resource?

A. factories

B. education

C. new technology

D. new machines

Use the timeline below to answer question 50.

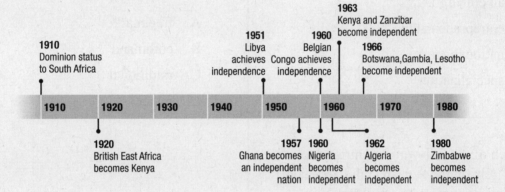

50. Which statement BEST represents the facts given in the timeline?

A. Most African countries achieved independence prior to 1940.

B. Most African countries achieved independence after 1950.

C. Most African countries are still European colonies.

D. The first African country to achieve independence was Kenya.

PLEASE GO ON TO THE NEXT PAGE.

POSTTEST

51. The deadliest natural disaster of all time was a flood on which river in Asia?

    A. Brahmaputra

    B. Huang He

    C. Indus

    D. Yangtze

52. Nigeria makes 80% of its export earnings from the sale of oil and gas. This is an example of

    A. an embargo.

    B. entrepreneurship.

    C. nationalism.

    D. specialization.

53. Which of the following countries does NOT rely on the Persian Gulf to transport its exports to world markets?

    A. Jordan

    B. Kuwait

    C. Iran

    D. Iraq

54. Which event led directly to the U.S. invasion of Afghanistan in 2001?

    A. al-Qaeda's September 11 terrorist attack

    B. Iraq's invasion of Kuwait

    C. Iran's attack on Iraqi oil fields

    D. Israel's withdrawal from the Gaza Strip

55. What kind of economy does South Africa use today?

    A. free market

    B. command

    C. traditional

    D. mixed

PLEASE GO ON TO THE NEXT PAGE.

POSTTEST

56. What was a positive impact of Europe's partitioning of Africa?

    A. civil wars

    B. new road construction

    C. separation of families

    D. separation of tribes

57. Which country promotes its major textile industry through efficient irrigation of the Indus River?

    A. India

    B. Pakistan

    C. Afghanistan

    D. Iran

58. Outsourcing is a new sector bringing employment to India's workers. Which major industry does outsourcing represent?

    A. services

    B. agricultural

    C. mining

    D. textile

59. In which part of the world is the lack of clean drinking water a major health problem today?

    A. Japan

    B. Sub-Saharan Africa

    C. Arabian Peninsula

    D. Turkey

60. Which of the following countries is NOT in Southwest Asia?

    A. Israel

    B. Iraq

    C. Saudi Arabia

    D. Vietnam

PLEASE STOP! DO NOT GO ON TO THE NEXT PAGE.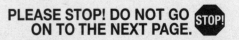

POSTTEST

Glossary

1973 oil crisis when OPEC announced that its member countries would stop exporting oil to countries that had aided Israel in its recent war with Egypt (Lesson 24)

38th parallel the line of latitude that separates North Korea from South Korea (Lesson 29)

acquired immunodeficiency syndrome (AIDS) a disease spread by HIV; the most severe health crisis in the world (Lesson 11)

African National Congress (ANC) founded in 1912, a group that wanted to bring people of all ethnicities together and fight for rights and freedoms (Lesson 6)

African Union (AU) an organization of 53 African countries that work together for peace and security (Lesson 7)

al-Qaeda a group of radical Islamic terrorists based largely in Afghanistan (Lesson 19)

ANC Youth League a group founded in 1944 by Nelson Mandela to bring a new generation to fight against racism and apartheid (Lesson 6)

anti-Semitism hostility toward or prejudice against Jews or Judaism (Lesson 17)

apartheid laws created to enforce segregation of people by race in South Africa (Lesson 5)

Arab a mixed ethnic group made up of people who speak the Arabic language (Lesson 10)

archipelago a chain of islands (Lesson 31)

Armenians an ethnic group that lives mostly in Armenia and the surrounding areas and are mostly Christian (Lesson 22)

armistice an agreement to stop fighting (Lesson 29)

Ashanti a group of people who live in central Ghana and believe in the Golden Stool (Lesson 10)

Asian Brown Cloud a brown haze that has many effects on the places it travels above; effects include altering monsoon patterns, increasing human respiratory problems, and reducing solar radiation (Lesson 32)

Atlas Mountains a mountain range that stretches from southwest Morocco to northern Tunisia (Lesson 8)

authoritarian a system of government in which the leaders control all of its aspects (Lesson 1)

autocratic government power lies in the hands of a single figure (Lesson 1)

ayatollah a recognized religious authority in Iran (Lesson 23)

Balfour Declaration a statement by Britain in 1917 that said Britain would work toward the establishment of a national home for the Jewish people in Palestine (Lesson 17)

Bantu a group that originally came from southeastern Nigeria and reached present-day Zimbabwe and South Africa, establishing the Munhumutapa Empire (Lesson 10)

Bedouin an ethnic group who speaks Arabic and used to be nomadic but now live mostly in Saudi Arabia, Syria, Jordan, and Iraq (Lesson 10)

Berbers a minority group in Southwest Asia who mostly live in North Africa and were the first group to settle that region (Lesson 22)

Berlin Conference a series of meetings in Berlin, Germany, held by European countries from 1884 to 1885, in which they decided how Africa's lands would be divided (Lesson 4)

bicameral a legislature with two houses (Lesson 34)

biogas a cooking fuel produced by breaking down organic matter (Lesson 32)

bourgeoisie landowners or factory owners who have power over the working class (Lesson 28)

Brahmans the highest caste, or priestly class, in Hinduism (Lesson 33)

Buddhism a religion that teaches the four noble truths and follows the Eight-Fold Path (Lesson 33)

budget a plan for spending and saving money (Lesson 2)

cabinet a group of people who advise the president and help run the government (Lesson 1)

calligraphy brush painting of Chinese characters on silk paper (Lesson 33)

capital goods any goods that are used to produce other goods (Lesson 14)

caste a class system (Lesson 33)

Christianity a belief that Jesus is the Jewish messiah. Its book is the Bible, which consists of the Hebrew Bible and other books in the Old Testament, and a New Testament, which includes Jesus's teachings. (Lesson 15)

civil war fighting between two or more groups or regions within the same country (Lesson 7)

civilian a person who is not part of the military of a country (Lesson 34)

coalition government a group of several different political parties that have to cooperate in order to make decisions (Lesson 23)

Cold War a struggle for world power between the United States and the Soviet Union in which there was no actual warfare (Lesson 29)

colonialism the forced control of one country by another country (Lesson 4)

command economy an economic system in which the central government decides which goods and services are needed and how they will be produced (Lesson 2)

compound interest earning interest on interest (Lesson 2)

confederation a voluntary association of states in which individual states hold more power than the central government. States agree to join together to form a central government, but each state retains the power to act independently. (Lesson 1)

Confucianism a philosophy and a way of life based on the life and teachings of Confucius (Lesson 33)

constitution a document stating the basic laws that govern a country (Lesson 1)

constitutional monarchy a government in which the head of state is a king or queen and in which the supreme law of the land is written in a constitution (Lesson 12)

consumer a person in an economy who buys and uses goods and services (Lesson 2)

credit money you borrow from a bank (Lesson 2)

crime against humanity an international law term that refers to a serious attack on human dignity or a grave humiliation or degradation of one or more human beings (Lesson 6)

Cultural Revolution Mao Zedong's attempt to close the gap that existed between the elite of the cities and the peasants of the countryside in China (Lesson 28)

currency a system of money (Lesson 3)

currency exchange rate compares one country's currency to another (Lesson 3)

deforestation the loss of forest land (Lesson 9)

demilitarized zone (DMZ) an area between North and South Korea (Lesson 29)

democratic government a form of government that relies on active citizen participation; voters choose their own leaders through elections (Lesson 1)

desalination a process for removing salt from salt water (Lesson 21)

desertification the transformation of usable land into desert (Lesson 9)

diaspora any people or ethnic group that must leave their homeland, and as a result become dispersed throughout other parts of the world (Lesson 7)

Diet Japan's parliament (Lesson 34)

diversified a larger number of different industries contribute to the country's economy (Lesson 14)

domino theory a belief that if one country fell to communism, then others in the area would follow just like dominoes falling over (Lesson 29)

Dreyfus Affair an incident in which a Jewish member of the French army, Alfred Dreyfus, was accused of spying for Germany. Although later found innocent, his initial imprisonment sparked anti-Semitic riots in Paris. (Lesson 17)

drought a severe absence of rainfall (Lesson 9)

Druze an ethnic group that is based on a religion that is a mixture of Islam and other religions. They live mostly in Lebanon and keep their religious practices secret. (Lesson 22)

Economic Community of West African States (ECOWAS) a pact made in 1975 among sixteen West African countries hoping to promote strength in the region, to raise the standard of living and stability in the region (Lesson 13)

economic sanctions policies such as trade restrictions and embargoes (Lesson 7)

economy the way in which people meet their needs through the production, distribution, and use of goods and services (Lesson 2)

embargo a ban on trade with a certain country (Lesson 3)

entrepreneur a person who takes the risk of organizing and running a new business (Lesson 14)

Ethiopian Highlands a rugged, mountainous region that covers parts of Ethiopia, Eritrea, and Somalia (Lesson 8)

ethnic group a cultural community of people with common ancestry, often sharing common religion, language, and traditions (Lesson 5)

export a product a country sends to another country (Lesson 3)

extraction the process of removing natural resources from the ground (Lesson 21)

famine when a region does not have enough food for a long period of time (Lesson 11)

federal system a form of government in which power is shared more evenly between the central government and the government of states or provinces (Lesson 1)

free trade trade without tariffs or other trade barriers (Lesson 3)

genocide the pre-planned murder of entire national, racial, political, or ethnic groups (Lesson 7)

government the system a country uses to make laws and run the country (Lesson 1)

Great Leap Forward a series of policies that Mao Zedong thought would help China become equal to the leading powers of the West in agricultural and industrial production (Lesson 28)

gross domestic product the total value of all the goods and services produced by a country each year (Lesson 14)

guerillas fighters who use hit-and-run tactics when fighting rather than traditional fighting methods (Lesson 30)

haiku a form of unrhymed poetry of three lines and a specific number of syllables per line (Lesson 33)

hajj a pilgrimage to Mecca (Lesson 33)

Hamas an Arab group, supported by Syria and Iran, based in the West Bank and Gaza Strip that has led attacks on Israel (Lesson 18)

Hezbollah an Arab group from Lebanon supported by Syria and Iran that has led attacks on Israel (Lesson 18)

Hinduism a polytheistic religion in India which divides society into castes (Lesson 33)

Ho Chi Minh Trail a system of paths through the jungles and mountains that connected North Vietnam to South Vietnam via Laos and Cambodia (Lesson 30)

Holocaust Hitler's attempt to rid Earth of Jews by large-scale, systematic murders (Lesson 17)

homelands poor, crowded areas far away from cities where blacks were forced to live in South Africa (Lesson 6)

human capital the value of people's work (Lesson 14)

human immunodeficiency virus (HIV) the virus that causes AIDS (Lesson 11)

import a product a country buys from another country (Lesson 3)

import quota a limit on the number of goods that can be imported from a certain country (Lesson 3)

income money that comes in or is earned on a regular basis (Lesson 2)

infrastructure the public system of services of a country (Lesson 27)

interest a charge a bank pays you to use your money (Lesson 2)

investing spending money in the hope of earning more money than is spent (Lesson 2)

Islam a religion based on the belief that a prophet, Muhammad, had a vision of an angel who gave him messages from God. Its book is the Qur'an. The faith is based on five pillars. (Lesson 15)

Israel an independent state that was created from lands in Palestine (Lesson 17)

jingxi in China, a drama of the capital city (Lesson 33)

Judaism the oldest of the three major religions in Southwest Asia. It began as a set of beliefs and laws practiced by ancient Hebrew people. Its book is the Hebrew Bible. Jews believe that one day a human leader will come as a messenger of God and bring about a golden age. (Lesson 15)

Kabuki theater Japanese drama about historical events or love relationships (Lesson 33)

kami spirits that control all the forces of nature, in Shinto (Lesson 33)

Knesset the Israeli legislature (Lesson 23)

Kurds a group in Southwest Asia that lives in several different countries, including Turkey, Syria, Iraq, and Iran, and whose religion is a mixture of several religions (Lesson 22)

Law of Return a law in Israel that states that a Jew from any other country can automatically have citizenship in Israel (Lesson 22)

literacy rate the percentage of people that can read and write (Lesson 11)

Long March a dangerous journey made by the Communists in China in 1934 (Lesson 28)

luxury something we want but do not need (Lesson 2)

malaria a tropical disease spread by mosquitoes (Lesson 11)

market economy an economic system managed by the people, based on supply and demand (Lesson 2)

Marxism a political philosophy that focuses on class struggle (Lesson 28)

Mau Mau a secret society in Kenya which operated from 1952 to 1960 (Lesson 5)

missionary a person who goes to a foreign country to spread his or her religion (Lesson 4)

mixed economy a system in which people are free to control the means of production. Individuals and businesses decide what to produce, how to produce it, and how much it should cost. The government also regulates the economy. (Lesson 2)

monsoon a pattern of seasonal winds that return every year in Southern Asia (Lesson 31)

nationalist movement a movement that seeks independence for the people living in a country (Lesson 5)

necessity something people need (Lesson 2)

New Imperialism the end of the 19th century when there was fierce competition between European countries for land and power (Lesson 4)

Nile River the world's longest river, in Africa (Lesson 8)

nirvana the freeing of the self from material desires (Lesson 33)

nomadic people people who move from one place to another in search of food and water for themselves and their herds (Lesson 10)

nonviolent resistance a form of political protest that does not use force or violence (Lesson 26)

oligarchic government a system in which an unelected powerful group uses its hold over the government to enrich itself and deny power to the citizens (Lesson 1)

Organization of Petroleum Exporting Countries (OPEC) an international organization that has twelve members and whose goal is to keep the price of oil as stable as possible (Lesson 24)

Ottoman Empire an empire that began in 1299, in Turkey, and grew to include parts of Southwest Asia, Africa, and Europe (Lesson 16)

outsourcing hiring people in other countries and paying them lower wages to do certain types of work (Lesson 36)

Pacific Rim the countries that border the Pacific Ocean (Lesson 35)

Palestine Liberation Organization (PLO) a group made up of several Palestinian political groups in different countries who are united in their goal of taking back Palestine from the Israelis (Lesson 18)

Pan-Africanism the idea that there is a global African community made up of native Africans and the descendants of African slaves and migrants across the world (Lesson 7)

pandemic a widespread epidemic (Lesson 11)

parliamentary system a form of government in which the executive branch is not as independent of the legislative branch as it is in a presidential democracy. The leader of the government is usually the prime minister. (Lesson 1)

Persians an ethnic group that has lived in Iran since before the arrival of Islam in the 7th century. They have their own language called Persian, or Farsi. (Lesson 22)

pogroms violent, anti-Jewish mob attacks (Lesson 17)

presidential system the executive branch is headed by the president, while the legislative branch is headed by Congress. The president is independent of Congress. (Lesson 1)

prime minister the leader of the government in a parliamentary system (Lesson 1)

puppet state a government set up in a country that is actually run by an outside country (Lesson 28)

qin a long seven-stringed zither, a Chinese musical instrument, that is plucked with the fingers (Lesson 33)

racism the belief that one type of ethnicity is better than another (Lesson 6)

refining making oil from the ground ready to make fuel to operate machines (Lesson 21)

reforestation planting trees in order to restore a forest (Lesson 9)

representative democracy a system of government in which the people elect representatives who act on their behalf (Lesson 12)

republic a system in which citizens elect leaders to represent them (Lesson 12)

Sahara the world's largest desert, in Africa (Lesson 8)

Sahel a strip of semi-arid land south of the Sahara Desert (Lesson 8)

samsara life's cycle of death and rebirth (Lesson 33)

savannah a large tropical grassland with scattered trees, in Africa (Lesson 8)

saving setting money aside for later use (Lesson 2)

Scramble for Africa the growth of European colonies in Africa (Lesson 4)

Shinto Japan's native religion that has neither sacred writings nor an organized set of beliefs or even a founder (Lesson 33)

Southern African Development Community (SADC) nine South African countries came together in 1980 to form a treaty that assists in making government and monetary policies for its members (Lesson 13)

specialization a country produces goods that it is able to make efficiently (Lesson 3)

spend to pay money for things you need (Lesson 2)

stalemate when no side claims victory (Lesson 29)

subsistence farming a method of farming in which nearly all of the crops or livestock raised are used to maintain the farmer and the farmer's family, leaving little, if any, surplus for sale or trade (Lesson 8)

Suez Canal a human-made trade route between Europe and Asia (Lesson 4)

sultan the ruler of a Muslim state (Lesson 16)

Swahili a group of people, who live on the East African coast from southern Somalia to northern Mozambique, who practice a strict form of Islam (Lesson 10)

Taoism a philosophy in China. In Chinese, *tao* means "the way." The way represents the flow of life. (Lesson 33)

tariff a tax on imports (Lesson 3)

theocracy a government run by religious leaders (Lesson 23)

trade the exchange, purchase, or sale of goods and services (Lesson 3)

trade balance the difference in value between a country's imports and exports (Lesson 4)

trade barrier something that limits what a country can trade and to whom (Lesson 3)

trade deficit when a country imports more than it exports (Lesson 13)

trade surplus when the value of a country's exports is greater than its imports (Lesson 13)

traditional economy an economic system based on traditions, routines, and beliefs (Lesson 2)

transnationalism legally living and working in more than one country (Lesson 35)

triangular trade a pattern of trade that occurred between Europe, the Americas, and Africa (Lesson 4)

tropical rainforest a dense evergreen forest with an annual rainfall of at least 60 inches (Lesson 8)

Turks an ethnic group based on the Turkish language who mostly live in Turkey and Iran (Lesson 22)

unicameral a legislature with one house (Lesson 34)

unitary system a form of government in which the central government decides which powers to grant to local governments. Local governments have important powers, but these powers are not clearly defined by the country's constitution. (Lesson 1)

Viet Cong a group of Communists in South Vietnam who sought reunification of Vietnam under Communist rule (Lesson 30)

Viet Minh nationalist and Communist forces in Vietnam (Lesson 30)

Vietnamization the policy of turning over control of the Vietnam War to South Vietnam while U.S. troops withdrew (Lesson 30)

water rights agreements about how countries can use the water in a region (Lesson 21)

weapons of mass destruction (WMDs) chemical or biological weapons (Lesson 19)

westernized to become more like Europeans or Americans (Lesson 26)

Zionism a Jewish movement that began in Europe in the late 19th century to establish a Jewish homeland in Palestine (Lesson 17)

Notes